NO EASY ANSWERS

This book is available

to borrow

from the

Primley Church Library

About the co-author

Christine Leonard lives in Surrey with her husband and two children. She is a freelance writer whose biographies include *A Giant in Ghana* published by New Wine Press and *Expecting the Impossible* (for children) published by Scripture Union.

No Easy Answers

**Lou Lewis
with Christine Leonard**

KINGSWAY PUBLICATIONS
EASTBOURNE

ISBN 0 85476 356 2

Produced by Bookprint Creative Services
P.O. Box 827, BN23 6NX, England for
KINGSWAY PUBLICATIONS LTD
Lottbridge Drove, Eastbourne, E Sussex BN23 6NT.
Printed in Great Britain

This book is dedicated to
my husband Steve and my family,
past and present.

Acknowledgements

Many of the key people in my life are mentioned in the following pages, and I would like to thank publicly those who offered, sometimes sacrificially, ongoing care and support.

My grateful thanks go to my prayer group, Bridget, Ruth and Margaret; to our support team, Pete and Pam Cousins, Geoff and Anne Hughes, Faith Russell, and Phil and Ian from Lighting Sound Services; to the nannies who have looked after our children so we could look after everything else; to John Paculabo, who has always had a vision for my music and ministry; and to Andy Hague, John Willett and Steve Le Maistre, whose commitment and help over the years is incalculable.

I would like to thank Stuart and Jayne Lindsell, Carol Gemmell, Bill Hatfield and Pam MacKenzie for their help with the manuscript, and John, Philip and Hannah Leonard for their patience during the writing process.

Contents

Introduction

This is my story *as I remember it*. As the narrative unfolds it will become obvious that during certain phases of my life a clear perspective was not always possible (or even desired!). I may have overlooked some pertinent details and over-emphasised others, but I have truly tried to recount this story with honesty and clarity. The result will inevitably be remembered fragments of my life rather than an objective and perfect overview.

For obvious reasons to do with protecting confidentiality, some names have been changed.

Lou Lewis

I

Precipice

The school of life, it taught me how to hide,
Structurize and fantasize and run away inside,
To drown my sorrows in nicotine and wine
That undermined my body and disturbed my mind.

I still remember it. The pull towards the edge of the cliff. The void. The noise in my head. Even now any loud continuous noise—a drill, a tube train—and I feel the panic rising. If I'm not careful I spiral down into a black hole of nothingness and I am alone again—a tiny speck in a huge and hostile universe.

It had seemed like a good idea at the time—a weekend by the sea. Jon knew this couple who had rented a big house in St Margaret's Bay near Dover. He'd bring the dope and the four of us would have a laugh. I liked the idea of playing hippy communes for the weekend—peace, love and all that. It was early 1970.

The house looked large and imposing, standing in its own grounds, though we found quite a mess indoors. That first evening we all sat round eating a take-away, tin foil lids everywhere. Mike and Susan seemed close, and though probably not married, must have been together for a while, I thought. With his long, blond hair Mike reminded me of a hopeless poet. I wanted him.

And so it started—the sidelong glances, the 'accidental' touch of fingers as I cleared away the remains of congealing chow mein. Mike made some comment about my dress and gently brushed my head as he passed—enough to spark off the old fantasy of secret, forbidden passion. A hopeless love affair! I savoured the drama of it all. It gave me a quick buzz of satisfaction to win these little games, proving to myself that I could take someone else's man and then control him. I enjoyed possessing men, making the things I liked about them part of me. Maybe we could do something artistic together, I day-dreamed. Paint? Write? *'You must meet Mike and Lou—such a talented couple!'* I could almost hear people saying some time in the future.

Jon guessed where I had been during the night and cursed me. He tended to mumble strange incantations and kept weird symbols in his flat and around his neck. That morning I laughed inside at his cursing and anger. I thought I had talked him round by the time he distributed the LSD, so I'll never know if he gave me neat liquid on purpose. As well as the carefully diluted variety which we always used, he did have a bottle of undiluted with him. As little as a hundred-millionth of a gram of that stuff will send you on a trip lasting for eight to ten hours.

Certainly, from the moment the drug started taking effect, I realised that something was badly wrong. We were walking on the cliff path. I liked being outside when I'd taken drugs so that I could observe the landscape shifting and changing as it took on transcendental significance. This time it did that with a vengeance. The world grew obscenely gigantic, while I shrank, ever smaller and more insignificant. But unlike Alice, stumbling into her Wonderland, I felt grotesquely afraid. I seemed to hang in time and space, alone. The vast universe which now surrounded me appeared unfriendly—no, actively hostile. I felt lonelier than ever before—a cosmic loneliness. All the time panic was rising, taking possession of me.

The cliff edge crumbled a couple of paces away. Beyond that grey sea, cold and formless, met grey sky. I felt myself being drawn towards the cliff, towards oblivion where the foaming sea smashed against a rattle of unfeeling pebbles. Fear pumped my heart as the pull grew stronger—a tangible pull towards the edge of nothingness, the empty vortex. I must have been nearly over the edge when I felt Jon grab my shoulder roughly, spinning me round, pushing me away from the sheer drop.

'I'm taking you back to the house,' he shouted, full in my face. I began to put one foot in front of the other as he propelled me forward. But although the immediate danger of hurling myself into oblivion had passed, the panic attack intensified with every breath and with every pounding heartbeat.

We staggered up the hill negotiating a series of steps with level stretches in between. I could feel my legs carrying me along, but a shutter slammed in my brain splitting mind from body. My vision narrowed to a still picture of my foot on the first step, though I had in reality reached the top of the flight. And then the nightmarish vision would click to another still picture, not of where I stood at that moment, but of a different place where my foot had been. A continuous whirring noise deafened me. I thought it would drive me literally mad, because it came from inside my head, which meant I could not escape.

Back at the house I drowned myself in music. Pounding tracks shook the building for hours, masking those unbearable whirring sounds just a little. I held Jon's hand. 'Tell me you love me, tell me you love me,' I pleaded, endlessly, although I knew he could never really love me.

'I love you, I love you,' he murmured. We both knew I didn't want his love, his commitment. I could only hope that this pantomime might draw me back from insanity.

The intensity of my panic attack began to lessen a little after fourteen hours. I can remember sitting staring at the squares on the grille of a gas fire. They made a pattern. As I curled up in the warmth of that fire I began to find some measure of relief. But on the train back to London, the view from the windows seemed unutterably bleak and I suspected then that my life would never be the same again. I knew that the fear which had opened up like a horrible chasm would stay with me. I had laughed at fear right through my teenage years, but now a drug had unleashed it within me. I did not know what to do. It had taken me over, its power was more real than anything I had known before. The comfortable view, which I used to hold, had me at the centre of the universe in control of my world. No one and nothing else mattered much. But now I realised that my sense of power had been an illusion. I was not in

control at all—not in control of my world and not in
control of myself. Maybe I never had been.

Back in London, Jon said the solution was simple.
'People sometimes have bad trips on LSD because
it's a synthetic drug. Go back to the same place and
do a re-run—this time on mescaline.' Jon assured
me that taking this more natural form of drug which
contains similar chemicals to LSD would somehow
over-write the horrors of my bad trip with pleasant
experiences. I tried. True, it did not reach the epic
dreadfulness of the previous time but the panic, the
whirring noise, the mind-bending flashbacks to feelings of cosmic loneliness were still beyond bearing.
Though I never took drugs again, I had left it too
late. From then on flashbacks interrupted my everyday life, paralysing me. I was falling apart, losing all
control, all sense of stability, even during my regular
week at college.

I'd always had my super-cool image to hide
behind—my clothes, my cynicism, my escapes into
drugs and fantasy. I had so excelled at becoming the
person I wanted to be that I had even fooled myself.
I was so good at hiding my feelings behind a permanent mask that I never realised they existed. I had
always managed to get what I wanted through
manipulating people—and men in particular—so I
suppose that explains why it took a bewildered look
from a man to make me realise that I needed help. I
saw a reflection of myself in the reaction of his eyes.
He didn't respond to my 'come on' signals. He didn't
know what to make of someone who was so evidently
falling to pieces.

By now the one person I really loved had dropped
out of my life and I had never allowed myself to get

close enough to anyone else to show them any need or weakness I might have. Part of the reason why I turned to Cherith for help was that I sensed she had been genuine and consistent in her offer of friendship. Goodness knows why my pocket contained Cherith's phone number written on a scrap of paper. She must have asked me to some Christian event, brave girl. When I phoned her home near Clapham Junction she dropped everything and rushed across London to find me. I must have looked a sight— thin, hollow-eyed, dressed in black from head to toe. I'd even picked up an infestation of scabies.

So I did not expect what I saw in Cherith's eyes. I saw faith. Faith in God, yes, though I would not have recognised that then. But I couldn't get over the realisation that she had faith in me—and for me! She held out hope and became the first person to give me confidence that...perhaps...things could change.

They did, in time. And it would make a nice tidy end to the story to say something like, 'Cherith's Jesus waved a magic wand, my nightmare turned into a Wonderland, I met a handsome vicar, had 2.4 splendid children and we all lived happily ever after!' But I've kissed goodbye to fantasies, new and old, and the truth is not that simple.

The final trip on LSD was so terrible that it did bring my life to a crisis and a turning point. But I had to choose to face the pain which had brought me to that place—the pain which had caused me to become both damaged and destructive. That alone took years.

This book tracks my journey towards wholeness, which has held its own joys and agonies. But if you are to understand what happened later, I must begin at the beginning...

2

Heartache

A mother's heart is a beautiful thing,
Terribly tender and easily broken;
I was amazed at the feelings inside
As I lay and I gazed at my newborn child.

The balcony of a big London hospital provided the
stage for my first public performance—a strange
setting for anyone's birth! Even from conception it
had been drama all the way. A bout of rheumatic
fever, years earlier, had left Mum's heart damaged
and pregnancy put a huge strain on it. She had
passed out during a long and traumatic labour before
giving birth to my older brother Paul, and took a
long while to recover afterwards.

Some people would have followed medical advice
and remained satisfied with one much-loved son, but
my parents longed for another child, a girl if possible.
Devout Christians, they asked God to keep Mum
safe while she had another baby. After two early
miscarriages, the medics gave her treatment to prevent another loss, and in 1951 I was on the way.

'Do you *really* want this baby?' asked a worried

heart specialist at the London teaching hospital.
'Definitely!' replied Mum, whose bump was hardly
beginning to show four months into the pregnancy.
She had to rest in a hospital bed for weeks. Sometimes they even forbade her to wash herself. But they
said the baby was doing fine and that good news kept
her going.

Just a few days before my birth she sneaked a look
at her hospital notes. Her heart started thumping as
she read that her GP had ordered her original visit to
the hospital not to arrange the best possible care for
herself and the baby, as she had always supposed.
He had in fact suggested a termination of the pregnancy because of Mum's 'very suspect' heart. Mum
showed typical determination as she prayed for a safe
delivery and for at least twelve years in which to
bring up her children.

Her contractions started on the morning of the
14th of March and she had reason to thank God that
it was a Wednesday. Hard and fast rules in those
days allowed husbands to visit only in the evenings—plus Wednesday and Saturday afternoons.

'I'll be much worse when you see me next,' Mum
told Dad at the end of afternoon visiting that day. By
the time he came back in the evening she was too ill
even for the gas and air which would have numbed
her pain a little. She gasped and struggled for air in
the stuffy ward and found breathing easier when they
moved her bed onto the balcony outside. 'How much
longer?' Dad asked the midwife. But despite the
pain, Mum had made little progress.

'Go home and try to get some rest, Mr Hayles, she
won't have this baby before the morning.' Dad
looked at his watch—8.30! Her heart can't hold out

much longer, he agonised. How could he possibly
rest? He dived into a telephone kiosk outside the
hospital. But instead of dialling a number to make a
call, he prayed. After a while such a deep peace
flooded through him that, much to his own surprise,
he slept soundly that night.

At nine o'clock (the very time when Dad had been
praying) Mum felt something happening. Panting
and sweating in her balcony bed, she shouted for a
nurse. Before anyone reached her, I was taking my
first gulps of cool night air. Horrified medics
swooped me out of the unsterile sheets. Then, on the
principle of 'better late than never', they rushed
Mum up to the delivery room. Some time passed
before a harassed nurse informed her, 'It's a girl!'
My parents named me Linda Christine—'Lou'
came later.

'This lady works miracles!' Mum overheard the
heart specialist whisper to the obstetrician next day.
Before she could counter, 'I don't work miracles, but
God does!' the white-coated specialist spoke to her
severely, *'No more babies!'*

Mum needed rest and time to recover. The hospital did not allow her to feed me and, on the few
occasions when they brought me to her, she worried
about my transfer from the jungle heat of the nursery
to the arctic conditions of her outside balcony. Terrified that I would catch cold, she wrapped me tight
in her bed jacket and so never noticed sores running
red-raw on my fingers and bottom. Busy staff with a
nursery full of crying babies had overlooked such
details.

When the hospital finally let us home my parents
wanted to thank God in public—because they

believed that he had brought their whole family safely through an anxious time. They were very involved in the local Baptist church. Baptists never baptise or 'christen' babies, because they believe that a person should be old enough to make up his or her own mind about such an important step. Instead, they 'dedicate' babies to God. The service thanks God for giving the little one 'safely and wholly'. My parents said those words with full hearts. Because they felt that God had intervened so that I could be born, they also wondered if he might have a particular purpose for my life.

I have always known how much my parents wanted me and that my birth had something special about it. But although they loved me dearly, Mum remained weak in health. She could pick up a tiny baby without much difficulty but, as I grew bigger and heavier, the doctor advised her that this would put too great a strain on her heart. Dad worked as a policeman, and later as assistant pastor of a large Baptist church in Croydon, both of which left him little time for the family.

When I was two, our next-door-neighbour suffered a heart attack. Mum left me to attend to her—literally for ten minutes. My first conscious memory is of sitting on the stairs that day, petrified because she had gone. Then I put on my hat and coat and struggled to open the front door in a desperate attempt to reach her. For weeks afterwards I hardly slept. I kept waking, screaming and kicking, from nightmares. Our doctor prescribed a course of phenobarbitone—the only measure he knew to calm me.

A few years later I travelled with Mum to an appointment at Guy's Hospital in London. On the train home she became feverish and I could see she was in great pain. I was only eight years old and had no idea what to do. I felt the panic rising again. Eventually we discovered that she had penicillin poisoning.

These dramatic events only served to reinforce the everyday fear which I felt of losing her. If ever my parents left us with a babysitter for the evening, I would wait for them anxiously. Once they were delayed by a road accident. I paced to and from the garden gate in the thick London fog, while my brother Paul played quite happily inside the house. Separations happen in this life and not always through cruelty and neglect, certainly not in my case. They say that we pick up adults' anxieties during our childhood, even in the womb. I certainly realised from early on that the world could be a tough place. Years later I wrote a song for someone much worse off than myself, someone who had not been wanted or loved as a child. But my own experiences helped me identify with the way she felt.

> You say that love is all I need,
> But love's an ache that has made me bleed,
> And you say that arms can comfort pain
> But I looked for arms and looked in vain.
> I run from dreams of people dying
> With no one there to take their place.
> And the world was cold when I was crying
> So I hid my tears behind an empty face.

It was years before I was able to work through some of these things and find the answer which appears in the last part of this song—to be able to apply it to myself and even help my friend. But that story will take more time to tell.

In the main I had a happy childhood. Mum is creative, highly intelligent, and although she may be limited physically, she makes up for that in drive and determination. Dad is warm and giving—and I adored him. Looking back, they must have had a struggle. We lived in a flat at first. Its oil stoves, as well as giving precious little heat, always worried my parents from the safety point of view. Mum had to wash all our nappies in cold water—and heaven knows how she dried them! The flat below ours hopped with fleas—and we shared a common passageway. Mum would rush Paul and me through it, but she only found out if we had attracted the unwelcome creatures when we sat on our potties— whereupon any present would drop into the contents!

I was two years old when we moved to a semi-detached house with a garden. One day Mum heard my screams while hanging out the washing and raced into the house to find me dangling out of my cot by one leg. What I must have done to her bad heart! One of those fearsomely active toddlers, I would tear round the house doing everything I knew to be forbidden. After a few hours of this Mum would resort to leaving me in my playpen, where I chattered away to my toys, quite safe and content. But as soon as I heard my Dad leaning his bike against the wall on his return home from work, I would let loose my most pitiful wails. Mum wilted under Dad's reproachful looks. Fancy allowing the little cherub to distress herself like that all day!

Even as a child I realised that we were poor—

assistant pastors earned a pittance. My brother and I knew our parents made sacrifices for us though, like all children, we constantly demanded things. Desperate for desks of our own, we jumped up and down in ecstasy when two appeared in our rooms one Christmas. My father had assembled them from kits but we could not have been more thrilled had they been made of solid gold.

I liked school—except for the hour's sleep which the reception class teacher forced on us after lunch! But once I came home really upset. Everyone wore a pleated gym-slip to infant school—everyone except me! And now I had been chosen to conduct the school's percussion band. Mum found an old pair of Dad's grey trousers, dyed them navy, then spent an entire night joining all the seams neatly under each box pleat. My gym-slip looked as good as anyone's when she had finished. A little later on I wore it to conduct the bands of several schools in the Croydon area during a combined concert.

I quite enjoyed wearing the inevitable hand-me-down clothes until I reached the age of about ten when it began to dawn on me that other families seemed to have more money to spend than ours. Why should we settle for a sagging yellow sofa which someone had passed on to us, even if it was a vast improvement on our previous moth-eaten green one? Why did my friends eat crisps every day when we could never afford them?

The middle-class standards which prevailed in those days must have added to our parents' strain. The children of good mothers always looked immaculate—while I plotted all day long to avoid having my long hair brushed. Though for years I never appreciated the true cost of my parents' love, as a child I did try to win their approval and achieve all the things that I thought they wanted. I knew Mum had been robbed of opportunities by her illness and because she had grown up in the War. And her family had not allowed her to take up a scholarship which she had won as a girl. In some way I longed to make those things up to her.

Nevertheless, although I had a keen sense of right and wrong, I began shoplifting in a mood of resentment at our lack of money. I grew quite skilful at it— until the day the owner of the local sweet shop spotted my antics. I felt dreadful. Back home I knew I had to tell Mum and she took me straight back to the shop to apologise. I never dared cross its threshold again even though I had to walk for miles to buy sweets elsewhere. The shame prevented me from shoplifting for years....

We had good times on holidays spent as a family with my grandparents in Worthing. Dad would transport Paul down there on his motor bike, while Mum and I took the train. Then Dad used his machine to carry us all around the South Downs. First he would take Paul riding pillion, then come back for me and finally for Mum—and so on, by stages. I found this enormous fun. I also remember spending hours roller-skating with Paul round Worthing's streets of retirement bungalows.

At one point Mum found secretarial work. For the first time we were able to buy things—like a Dansette record player, some classical records, and even a little Austin A30 car with an indicator which stuck out like a tiny semaphore arm.

I had a vivid imagination. A picture of the black

hole of Calcutta in Granny's big red encyclopaedia gave me nightmares. Tender-hearted and sensitive, I would cry at stories on *Children's Hour* and worry about poor Red Indians shot by cowboys. When a Sunday school teacher told us how a child prayed while bombs were falling all around her in the War, she intended the story to emphasise the way God kept the girl safe, but this moral failed to register with me. For the next few weeks I jumped in terror at any loud noise, despite the fact that the War had ended well before my birth. When we finally acquired a little black and white television, I remember laughing at Charlie Drake the very first time we watched it. But my most vivid recollection centres around the lasting terror I felt at the film *Quatermass and the Pit*. It would seem a tame science fiction tale by today's standards, but my imagination worked overtime on the first episode so my parents forbade me to watch the next instalment. I lay upstairs in bed, listening to the music, inventing my own plot, probably a hundred times more petrifying than the real thing.

My earliest memories of church are of playing with my brother in the back of the huge Baptist buildings in Croydon while we waited for Dad to finish some midweek duties. The endless rooms made me feel small. I was scared by their emptiness and musty smells, the creaks and echoes. I enjoyed singing hymns on Sundays, though. People at church spoilt me sometimes, which I liked. On the other hand, not wanting to be seen to favour the pastor's daughter, leaders rarely gave me the honour of carrying the flag in Girl's Brigade parades—something I really longed to do.

One night a whole group of us kids from West Croydon Baptist Church went to a Billy Graham rally. When Dr Graham invited people to come out and give their lives to Jesus, intense whisperings ran along our row. Should we go forward? If so, it had to be all of us, no one would dare go alone! In the end the whole row of us trooped to the front, joining a great tide of other people. But I can't say the experience made much difference to my life. If I believed in God it was because he was so real to Mum and Dad.

Paul and I spent hours at home playing services. Paul mimicked the preachers who came to our church, while I played an imaginary organ. I had started piano lessons quite young with the lieutenant of the Girl's Brigade. Dad played the violin well, so perhaps I inherited my love of music from him. I had an insatiable appetite for new pieces and gained good grades in piano exams. I must have shown promise, because Mum entered me for local festivals from the age of seven. They afforded good training in performing and in overcoming nerves and I enjoyed the experience. Though I rarely won outright, my name usually appeared among the top few. I did gain a silver medal and a cup for sight-reading, although I was by far the youngest in my class.

Then, when I reached the age of eleven, my parents told me some exciting news—we were moving, far away, to the country—to the seaside!

3

Playing the Clown

A child's heart is a beautiful thing,
Needs lots of loving but it does lots of giving!

In 1962 my family moved to Sidmouth on the south
coast of Devon. My parents explained that they
believed God had called Dad to become pastor of a
small church there. Though we would have a manse
to live in, the church could not pay anywhere near
enough to support us, so we would have to depend on
God to provide us with enough money to live on.

We jammed ourselves into our tiny Austin A30
car, piling luggage on its roof and cramming more
possessions into every crevice. Eventually we arrived
in this nice, respectable seaside town and craned our
heads out of the windows for the first sight of our new
house. It seemed like a palace after the one in
Croydon—detached, with bay windows and a roof
which sloped grandly over its built-in garage. Unfortunately, it was situated at the top of steep hills, so
Mum remained marooned there most of the time.
She could walk down the hills, but her heart protested at the return journey.

From the ottoman in my new bedroom I could just catch a glimpse of the sea. I spent hours there reading Enid Blyton, graduating later to Jean Plaidy. The huge Bramley apple tree in our garden pleased Mum. We all helped pack the tangy fruit away in newspaper, and later we enjoyed the goodies she made with it. Though by February the mere mention of yet another apple crumble set us groaning!

As a suburban child arriving in Devon my first horror concerned cows. They came at me down the road, huge and strange as a herd of wildebeest. There were no pavements, so I had to push past them in the road. I managed—legs shaking, terrified by their sounds, their smell and their closeness.

On the other hand, Paul and I spent blissful summers' days digging on sandy beaches, or fishing in the rock pools on Sidmouth's sea front. A black and white puppy with the highly original name of Laddie joined the family and we walked this much-loved animal for miles over the hills. Once we surprised a stag in all its majesty on the moor, while in spring we chased rabbits through woods full of bluebells. Occasionally I reached the pinnacle of my aspirations and managed to beg a horse ride, while dreaming night and day of somehow acquiring my Very Own Pony.

I often missed the bus which should have taken me to school in Ottery St Mary, so my father would chase off in the car, overtaking and then waving the bus down, so that I could jump on board. Later I travelled by train, through the valley of the Otter, on a magical line later axed by the infamous Dr Beeching.

Hearing about education today makes me green with envy. I would have jumped at the chance to do

colourful projects, go on exotic school trips and take
'A' level drama! By contrast, our first domestic science lesson showed a class of eager twelve-year-olds
how to boil an egg. The teacher demonstrated extra-
ordinary ingenuity in spinning out this *Cordon Bleu*
extravaganza to a full forty minutes. At the end of the
day we were expected to carry home one egg which
we had boiled ourselves plus two pieces of bread and
butter—an excitement from which I never fully
recovered!

Five white lines ruled on the blackboard marked
out the school's music room from other classrooms.
Further clues lay hidden in the cupboard—one tam-
bourine, one triangle and thousands of copies of
Merry Tunes for Young Folk. These dog-eared books
emerged during music periods so that we could anni-
hilate ditties such as 'Nymphs and Shepherds Come
Away'. The cupboard also concealed a Dansette
record player, complete with records so scratched
that for years I thought Beethoven's Fifth went Di-
Di-Di Dum...Dum...Dum...Dum.... We had no
opportunity to learn a musical instrument at school,
but Mum found me some excellent piano teachers
locally and from the third form on I played the piano
in school assemblies. Our music teacher specialised
in the violin—not the ideal instrument on which to
accompany several hundred boys and girls chanting
'All Things Bright and Beautiful'!

I never quite felt I belonged at grammar school.
The most popular girls—the ones with the trendy
clothes who had boyfriends before the rest of us—
would tolerate me sometimes, but I never had the
freedom to do most of the things which they did

outside school. In a small town like Sidmouth everyone knew the Pastor's daughter. I might as well have
been living in a goldfish bowl! To me all women over
forty looked identical with their shapeless Crimplene
dresses, their sensible shoes and grey hair. I could
never recognise which 'old' person belonged to my
Dad's church and therefore might report back on my
misdeeds. I found myself constantly dodging around
corners or into doorways. 'What will the neighbours
think?' my mother always wanted to know. When
once I skipped out into the street barefoot, someone
had told Mum even before I ran back home again. So
my brother and I invented a new game. How much
could we do without Mum and Dad finding out?

We dreaded church people ringing the doorbell,
because we had to turn the television down and any
other plans we had as a family were instantly
shelved. While the visitors remained in our house,
our behaviour had to be strictly modified, as though
all minister's children came ready-supplied with
wings and haloes! God became equated in my mind
with someone who forbade most of the things which I
longed to do.

There must have been many fine people at the
church, but I found it convenient not to appreciate
them, nor to acknowledge anything which God
accomplished there. I did enjoy hymns and baptism
services. My father seldom gave a direct appeal for
people to come forward to give their lives to Jesus,
but he did at baptisms—while we all prayed like
mad that someone would respond. Once a little nine-
year-old boy made his way sobbing to the front of the
church and his father who was one of the deacons
proudly knelt beside his son, and hugged him. There

was hardly a dry eye in the place. Several of Paul's teenage friends became Christians and joined the church. Still it appeared to me, rightly or wrongly, that religious people had double standards and that Chistianity had more to do with appearances than with God's Spirit changing people from the inside.

I think Mum felt the strain of having to conform to other people's values most, for both my parents took a wider view on our behaviour than church members who had grown up in a stricter age. When, during my teenage years, my antics began to feature on the agenda at church leaders' meetings I sensed that, though Mum and Dad were prepared to give Paul and me a larger measure of freedom, inevitably the tension in the church limited what we were allowed to do.

I resented the church especially because, even though its numbers (and therefore its income) grew under Dad's ministry, it paid him so little. It cost too much to keep our house really warm, so we all shivered through the winters. One Christmas time some bottles of fizzy Corona, which we stored in the bay window of our parent's north-facing bedroom, froze solid. It became a family joke that Mum would dress in layers of clothes before going to bed, but I used to lie awake worrying when I heard her coughing at night. Although things did improve a little after the first few years, the conditions can't have helped her health and the church only installed central heating after Paul and I left home.

Still I had to admit that, when things became really desperate and my parents prayed, God did seem to come up with the goods. For example, when our washing machine broke down, Mum could never have managed the heavy loads by hand. We all prayed and a cheque arrived the next day which my Dad spent on a new machine.

When I reached fifteen some hippies from Eel Pie Island in London descended on Sidmouth for the summer. I thought them wonderful—free, bohemian and displaying just the required degree of dirtiness! (Though I did catch them, on more than one occasion, trooping off to the public toilets for a wash.) Once a policeman found me chatting up a group of them and concluded that I must be a young runaway. Terrified, I gave him a false name and address and then spent the whole afternoon dodging furtively about, convinced that the entire West Country police force had been called out to search for me. How would my parents cope with a daughter in jail? In the end I gave myself up at the tiny two-man police station and confessed my true identity. The constable had a twinkle in his eye as he gave me a lecture. He knew my dad. He knew that I knew he knew my dad—yet neither of us mentioned his name!

My first education in matters of love came from a magazine called *Jackie* whose typical heroine had zits. Her widowed mother struggled to bring her up along with eight siblings. By page three, however, the resourceful *Jackie* heroine rescued the son of the local mill owner from drowning. In gratitude he bought the girl her Very Own Pony. All that cantering around in the open air worked wonders for her complexion, whereupon the most attractive boy in class fell passionately in love with her—and they all lived happily ever after! I mainlined on such fantasy for two years and I really did believe that *it* would happen one day. Having spotted each other across a crowded room, something would draw us together, slowly, inexorably. As we brushed finger tips, ever so lightly, he would look into my eyes and say, 'Oh, what a beautiful girl! Tell me, what is your name?' 'Linda' hardly seemed worthy of the occasion. So in my imagination I would lisp, 'Arabella!' We would marry, live in a cottage with roses round the door and have ten children. Ten!!

My first real boyfriend, Alan, was thirteen. I was twelve. He paid homage to me by rushing bravely up the hill, depositing some sweets at my house and running away again, quite red in the face. Once he went so far as to proffer lipstick at which point my mother went off him. It hardly classed as a relationship anyway, since we never spoke more than a word, let alone went out together.

My first kiss happened behind the sports' pavilion at school. Snogging, we called it—a word straight out of *Collins Cave Man's Dictionary*! From the age of thirteen I became hooked on the opposite sex, which meant deceit grew ever more important. My parents would not let me near dances, or the cinema— nowhere around Sidmouth, anyway. I never felt I belonged—not to the church, which I despised for its hypocrisy, nor to groups of other young people in the town.

I could not remain an innocent romantic for long. I worked in a hotel one summer where the advances of the manager's son-in-law intrigued me. I led him on, not realising where exactly, until he started groping around my lower regions. I puzzled over why he showed such anger, as he accused me of first exciting then denying him.

Meanwhile I continued lighting up cigarettes behind trees, sneaking into pubs by the back door and generally rebelling against the restrictions of my upbringing. At one period I hung around Sidmouth's folk clubs listening to the long-haired singers with one finger stuck in their ear. After a couple of months it dawned on me that this aberration was not some secret code or problem with ear wax, it merely helped them to pitch notes. Another time I joined the Young Socialists, motivated as ever by the pursuit of attractive young men. Whenever I found one, I always knew my mother would ask—'Is he a Christian?' You must be joking, I thought. The moment boys started going to church they became boring, conventional and wouldn't want to do any of the things that I enjoyed most!

At the age of fifteen I really did fall in love. He was an artist of twenty-three. A real artist, freshly returned from America where he had won an award for his work. Fantastic looking, and impeccably dressed in a casual style, Nigel had a razor sharp wit and an easy-going temperament. Quite a catch in Sidmouth. I felt flattered that he even noticed me among the crowd at the Anchor pub. All the time he took me out I overflowed with happiness and I gave my love to him completely.

After a while he took me to bed, touching me gently, though he never attempted to take my virginity. Maybe he had considered the legal implications of having sex with a girl of fifteen. In any event, soon afterwards the landlord discovered my age and banned me from the Anchor. Nigel had to choose between me and his group of friends, and clearly for him there was no contest. So I lost my boyfriend and the crowd we went around with, all at the same time. I cried for about two weeks. Then I vowed that I would never let my real self, my deep emotions, become so involved in a relationship again. That way, I would avoid pain!

A few months later, at the age of sixteen, I left home. At last I would be free from the influence of church and family....

4

The Big, Wide World

Love has let me down,
I tried to play the game but it seems I have to lose.
Love has let me down
And a thousand dreams have turned to nightmares
   in my mind.
Why must love be unkind?

Before I left Sidmouth I walked along the sea front
and spat. 'Small-minded, small town,' I muttered, 'I
hate you!' Goodbye claustrophobic church and
home—it was 1967 and I was off to a residential Arts
College. I'd already seen some of the most fascinat-
ing people I had ever come across when I attended
my interview there.

The county of Devon awarded a few scholarships
each year for places at Dartington College of Arts.
What can I say to explain the place? The Champer-
nowne family built the Hall in 1559 and future gener-
ations lived there until 1925 when they hit hard times
financially. A millionaire, Leonard Elmhirst, bought
the estate from the family.

Elmhirst and his American wife gave the place an
unusual buzz. They knew Sir Rabindranath Tagore,

a Hindu poet and philosopher who while working for India's freedom tried to integrate Indian and Western culture. Elmhirst had helped Tagore set up an Institute of Rural Reconstruction in Bengal and carried his idealism back to Devon.

In 1931 Elmhirst set up the Dartington Trust, founding a co-educational school. Later Trust projects included businesses ranging from building and electrical to forestry, and from textile mills to shops. British people were persuaded to drink exotic things like apple juice way back in the thirties, while Dartington's model farm introduced artificial insemination of cattle to Britain. At the other extreme, the Amadeus String Quartet began at Dartington. Henry Moore and the potter Bernard Leach used to teach at the Arts Centre, and the Trust set up Dartington Glass Workshops at Great Torrington.

On the one hand Dartington represented a shining light at the end of the War. British politicians made pilgrimages there, observed and returned to Parliament to set up the Welfare State. On the other hand locals complained about the goings-on, muttering about communism, free love and strange Indian gurus. Because of its roots in the East, Dartington was into the New Age long before the term had been coined. Ravi Shanka gave a performance at the College during my time there and I learned to play the tabla, sitar and drums from an Indian teacher—very few other places in this country offered tuition in those instruments then.

Being musical had added to my sense of feeling 'different'—special, even. School appeared to attach little importance to music, so a teacher had suggested that I develop my talents elsewhere. At Dar tington the tuition and opportunities rated second to none. The scholarship gave me two years to study music and English to 'A' level, as well as practical singing and piano.

Dartington was in the same county as Sidmouth, but it felt like another planet to me. Most people at the College were around eighteen, while I'd gained a place at sixteen-and-a-half. What could be better? I had been given the sun, moon and stars rolled into one. I celebrated by buying the clothes of my dreams—purple cord trousers, an orange culotte dress with a long zip at the front, as many skimpy tops as possible, and hundreds of scarves, shawls and belts to complete the desired effect. Fashion-mad, I had managed to save quite a bit for my clothes-fund by working on Saturdays in Woolworths—especially as I had my fingers in the till. I also took holiday jobs as a waitress or chambermaid in local hotels, managing to enliven the boring tasks with dramatic scenes. For example, when one fussy boss indicated that I had not put the bedspread on correctly I threw it at her, yelled 'F*** the bedspread!' and stormed out of the hotel. Thus ended that job. I could only hope that my parents would never find out the real reason why.

When I arrived at Dartington, the Hall's sixteenth-century buildings basked in mellow September sunshine. But I only registered their serene beauty in passing. Instinctively my eyes homed in on the dreamy-looking blokes lounging around the place. When I was shown to my room, I realised that some of these heavenly male beings inhabited the same block. There weren't going to be many constraints here, I thought. No parents, no rules.

They laid on a disco that night to help new students get to know everyone. I couldn't believe the glittering array of wonderful, arty people—the summit of my desires. In Sidmouth fashion meant following the latest craze—one winter we all wore cloaks, for example. At Dartington, students created their own innovative look. The girl who later gave me the nickname Lindy-Lou was the first person I had seen wearing long clothes. Others went around with bare feet all the time. Trendsetters, I noticed, all came from the art and drama departments. Music students seemed dull by comparison and much more studious, probably due to all that practice. I avoided them.

A second-year student called Tim chatted me up. He wore a scarf round his neck, something I had only seen previously on little old ladies. I questioned him about the college and his answers confirmed my wildest dreams. 'So long as you go to lectures, you can pretty much do what you like here,' he yelled, struggling to make himself heard above the pounding disco beat. The more I found out the more I felt that this was the place for me—creative, *avant-garde*, free. Tim, with his unusual clothes, symbolised all I had ever wanted. He danced with me most of the evening, then invited me back to his room. Acceptance! Heaven! Innocent child, I jerked from my dream when I realised that he expected me to sleep with him.

'But Tim, I...well, we hardly know each other!' I stuttered. I could have handled anger at my refusal, or rejection, but not what I saw—mockery, laughter. Tim did not try to hide his amusement. Stifling my hurt, because I desperately needed to belong, I walked back to my room with head held high.

'I'll see you,' he called after me. Yes, of course. Why worry about a minor hiccup in the beginning of our relationship, I tried to convince myself. But those five minutes in Tim's room changed my life. Next morning he walked straight past me on the way to breakfast and sat with a group of friends. I waited for an invitation to join them. It never came. So the rules were different here. Well, I would play it their way, then.

As it turned out, my first sexual experience as a teenager came courtesy of a student from Exeter University—a decent bloke, though not one I knew well. I can't even remember his name.

'Why didn't you tell me?' he demanded, genuinely distressed, after we had made love. I failed to understand. What was the big deal? Everyone talked about IT—the great First Time—but IT hadn't felt that special to me! What on earth did they make all the fuss about? I was only playing by the new rules. In Sidmouth you fell in love. In Dartington you made love—and I made it with quite a few at College, including one of my tutors.

Dartington felt like enormous fun with very little hard work involved. At weekends we would all scream off in some outrageous car to the seaside. There we would consume cream teas and spend hours on the beach, making ourselves as conspicuous as possible.

Meanwhile, my Mum had given me a list of Christian contacts in the Dartington area. Needless to say I took great care that none of them ever found me. The College also had its very own Christian Union—a good target for jokes. How could they carry on with their ever-so-nice-and-narrow-ways in that wonderful, free-wheeling atmosphere? I almost crowed in triumph when the President of the Christian ghetto, who had been engaged to a pretty girl, left College a practising homosexual. All that hypocritical Bible-bashing would never work in a modern age!

Most of us students played around with the usual things—tarot cards, ouija boards, transcendental meditation. The soft drugs we used gave rise to their own weird occult symbolism. Spiritual hunger ran rampant, but as young artists we behaved like toddlers let loose in a store-cupboard, consuming anything we could find. Mustard, fairy liquid, biscuits, matches—who cared what?

My first dope came as another anti-climax. I noticed a cigarette about seven times larger than normal. People sitting in a room each took three puffs, then passed it on—very ritualistic. I did as most seventeen-year-olds would. But, though I drew deeply on the joint the regulation three times, I felt nothing, nothing at all. A whispered conversation confirmed that it did indeed contain the dreaded dope. School and parents, even the television, had portrayed drugs as terrible things, liable to leap out and ensnare you with certain death or, at the very least brain damage, the moment you so much as set eyes on them. Yet this stuff had less effect on me than a sniff of thin wine. So much for the authorities and their lying propaganda!

I knew all about getting drunk too. Most of my friends spent hours at the White Hart Pub in Dartington. I fumed at my exclusion, *still* too young. But that didn't stop me downing alcohol at another pub, the Cott. I learnt to time my drinking there so that I could still stagger the three-quarters of a mile of dark Devon lanes which led, uphill all the way, back to College.

Yet I never made myself blind drunk in order to escape. Why would I, when I'd found my dream at Dartington? I simply used drugs and alcohol as a recreational hobby at first, and also found them useful when under any pressure. I would down a few glasses or roll myself a joint and the happy haze made everything fine. I never needed to face up to my problems. I wasn't 'hooked', not physically. We used marijuana and cannabis, which appeared in no way the devils I had been led to believe. I could take care of myself without any of that boring stuff like effort and moral decisions. Who cared about growing into a responsible adult, anyway?

On my eighteenth birthday, the law of the land considered me mature enough to drink in the White Hart. I celebrated with eighteen scotches. Even my friends, who considered most excesses part of the norm, considered this one over-the-top—I was extremely sick afterwards. Often I drank to escape from myself for I hated being on my own. I still remember one poem I wrote at Dartington.

> Twisting, turning, longing to be free,
> My mind is locked in some dark deed of yesterday,
> A Domesday Book of all the deeds of Hell,
> Of happenings too terrible to tell
> And yet my mind remembers them so well.

What was I running from? What dark deeds? I didn't know. But one big question churned around in my mind—who was I? My place on the course proved that I had musical talent. Could the reason why I often felt different have something to do with a unique gifting? I'd fantasise about achieving fame and fortune through musical virtuosity.

I did love music, and the course proved brilliant, if laid-back. Our 'A' level tutor decided to change our syllabus half way through my second year, so I covered all the new course work in a few months—and still passed! I had fine training in piano, singing and, later, harpsichord. But now I know that I wasted many opportunities through my wild behaviour and certainly never worked with anything like the dedication needed to be the top class performer of my dreams.

Who was I? Others would tell me. If men fancied me, I must be desirable. If girls liked me, I must be popular. One girl stood out at College. It had nothing to do with her appearance. Her frizzy brown hair and the long yellow and black striped rugby shirt which she wore struck me as bizarre. But in a room full of students Anna's remarks made everyone laugh. She oozed wit and intelligence and had won the top award of the Associated Board of Music— their gold medal—for gaining the top marks in the country on her instrument.

At school I had always singled out the most popular girl in the class and tried to make sure she became my friend. The same happened here. I wanted whatever made Anna so special. If I could own her as my friend, maybe her talents and the parts of her personality which I so much admired would rub off on me. Funnily enough, it was Anna who first challenged me about the way I intermeshed fantasy with the real world. As she got to know me she said that she found it hard to distinguish whether I was lying or telling the truth.

With both men and women I acted brittle and vivacious and part of me knew that I made a fool of myself much of the time. Even the people I considered my friends found me difficult. One girl commented, 'You just use people!' and it dawned on me then that I might be inviting a widespread backlash of dislike. I resolved to act differently the next term, but I had honed to perfection all my little designs for getting what I wanted out of people, and changing these habits proved harder than I had imagined.

I spent all my time with people from College, plus the circle they attracted from outside. If I ever had to go home in the holidays I would endure the slow days before returning to my beloved Dartington again. But at least I *belonged* somewhere now. I could stroll around Sidmouth feeling superior in my loneliness, or better still shock religious old ladies as I posed with the latest imported boyfriend, specially selected for his fast car or enviable clothes.

In my last term part of our course took us to the pretty little harbour of Padstow in north Cornwall for their May Day celebrations. Beautiful sunny weather helped us to relax and enjoy the delightfully pagan ceremonies. Morris men with their sticks and hobby horses pranced through the streets, mingling with folk-worshippers who had travelled miles to attend. At the other extreme, local leather-clad bikers gravitated towards a fun fair which represented plastic technology at its worst. Most people, though, sat around outside pubs downing the pints of strong cider which seemed an essential ingredient of all folk festivals. The usual atmosphere of friendliness and well-being came largely, I suspect, from its effects.

Anna and I got very drunk and lay on a grassy hillside overlooking the harbour. The seagulls cried and some grass tickled my hand. I moved my hand across to Anna's and enjoyed the warmth of the touch. I realised that I didn't want to take my hand away and wondered what Anna would do. She seemed content, so we lay like that for a while.

I'd always gone for men. I might have been possessive of Anna as a friend, but had never noticed sexual overtones in my attraction to her. Now, on this grassy bank near Padstow, one thought led to another. I puzzled that if anyone had suggested anything of the kind a week earlier both of us would have laughed. Yet somehow it was happening—and I had made the first move. When we hitched a lift home a van picked us up and we huddled close in the darkness at the back, holding hands. I felt both appalled and excited.

When I was sober again next day, I wondered what I had done. I felt trapped because of our pre-existing friendship. I had vowed that I would never let any man get close enough to hurt me again. If one tried, I would always back off, hurling enough venom in the process to ensure that he never again tried to touch more than the skin of me. But this must be all right. I wasn't a lesbian, I couldn't be. Part of me refused to believe in this affair. The attraction wasn't primarily sexual. It had reached a physical level because each of us wanted to make the other feel good in an intense kind of way.

We spent most of our time together that term, hours and hours listening to music—passionate works like Wagner's *Tristan and Isolde* or the haunting *Sinfonietta* of Janacek. We tramped around pine woods which mirrored the dark intensity of the music. Fed by films about doomed lesbian love affairs, we existed within unreal romantic personas of ourselves, wrapped up in the bitter-sweet hopelessness of it all. Part of the attraction of our physical passion for each other lay in its secrecy—it seemed important that no one at Dartington found out. One of our tutors took Anna and me out to Becky Falls. We knew he was making a play for both (or either) of us, and we found it deliciously amusing to give him the slip in order to continue our own clandestine affair.

It hurt Anna that I still went out with men from time to time. I wasn't rejecting her, but merely, as usual, feeling confused about my identity. I thought it might help to prove myself bisexual rather than lesbian. But I could not compartmentalise my life, and really the affair with Anna dominated it completely. I have noticed how a man's objectivity often tempers a woman's emotional intensity. Many females find it harder to switch off, which may explain why love between two women can bind them together with such compulsive force.

One day Anna and I went into an empty church. I found a big old Bible on the lectern and started parodying some verses which condemned homosexuality. How we mocked and laughed and cursed. I no longer believed that God existed, so why should I care? But our love—compulsive, obsessive—ran very deep. Even when we fought, hurling vicious words at one another, we could not break free.

And we did fight. Anna had none of my excesses, my over-indulgence in drink or drugs. She worked hard at her music, playing in many orchestras, and she kept trying to reform me. She would try to discuss musical *motifs* and the finer points of harmony, but I never coped with music theory. She tried to organise my practice routine, but I hated anyone attempting to control me. In terms of personality we often annoyed each other. She thought of me as a pseud, obsessed with my external image. Her preoccupations lay in intellectual and spiritual realms. She believed that gods lived in trees and animals. The weasel, for some reason, held special significance—she ascribed magical powers to it. I failed to understand this side of her life at all.

That summer our courses at Dartington came to an end. The two years I spent there must rank as the most enjoyable in my whole life, before or since. Looking back, though, I think those same years also proved the most destructive. At the time I hated leaving and visited the college whenever possible, but never found it the same again. Now that my friends had gone, I felt an outsider.

5
Light Switch

Started well, had the world at my fingers
Didn't know I was chasing illusion
What do you do when everything becomes nothing
And then you find that the whole world starts
   running?

And there are times I remember your safety
And the times that you spoke to my heart
Now I see how wrong I can be
I'm coming, coming back home.

Anna and I both moved to London. Anna had a
place at the Royal Academy of Music and lived in
nearby Baker Street, while I attended the Royal
College of Music and shared a basement flat near the
Gloucester Road tube station. Anna lived in my
room at one stage—my flatmates embraced anything unconventional. One of the men would even
come and talk to us while we lay in bed, though
people at our colleges still knew nothing of our affair.

At that time my brother also lived in London, off
the King's Road. Jon, a friend of mine, rented the flat
alongside my brother's and lived by pushing dope.

We students were into reading Tolkien's *Lord of the Rings* at the time and I thought of Jon as Gandalf the wizard. Men with elf-like features didn't usually attract me, but image seemed all important and Jon projected an aura of hidden power. I saw him as an entrance to an intriguing world. For my nineteenth birthday Jon treated me to the biggest joint I'd ever seen. Then as our relationship began to develop he started supplying me with LSD. I made some kind of effort to practise my music and go to lectures during the week, but saw weekends as a time for myself, a counterfoil to the daily grind. I was often at a loose end on Saturdays and Sundays, because Anna was busy playing in orchestras, so I made drugs my relaxation. I escaped.

On my first LSD trip I 'found God'. He sat on the top of a pile, so by some strange logic he had to be God. Not that he was in the least important to me. With a pastor for a father I'd had enough of all that hypocritical church nonsense. No, I wasn't searching for God, or for friendship. I wasn't searching for anything, really—except stimulation and excitement. The attraction of Jon and his drugs was escape. Escape from stress and escape from myself into a world where realities shifted like the colours. A world full of drama—creative, new, exciting. A world where I could make my fantasies happen.

Often a group of us experimented to see how far we could go. After taking acid (LSD) we'd walk into a police station. Would they notice anything wrong? Even when I was having some weird, out-of-body experience, I still knew pretty much what was happening. I still kept control, or so I believed. Strange really, because some weekends blotted themselves right out of my memory. Occasionally I would find myself waking up somewhere like Notting Hill Gate, which even in those days was not a particularly safe place. Once someone almost dragged me into a basement before a passer-by came to my rescue. I never wondered if anyone 'up there' might be looking out for me. I guess I felt in my heart that anyone 'up there' would disapprove of my behaviour, so why would they be interested in me?

I suspected my mum of setting the college Christians on me. Their smiles made me shudder. How could they prance around with no inhibitions, singing their jolly, simplistic choruses? This wasn't a playschool and their immature behaviour appeared laughably uncool. Students of any degree of sophistication cultivated a moody look, expressive of sultry passion.

The pimply Christian guys appeared bad enough, all dandruff and NHS spectacles. But the clean, hard-working, ultra-friendly girls were always trying to buy me cups of coffee. I'm sure that some of them looked on me as their project—a sad case to be rescued. Fancy offering genuine kindness—how naive! Not that I minded the free coffee. Occasionally I'd play along and sit with them. Because of my background I knew the Bible inside out and found it amusingly easy to win arguments. I mocked them behind their backs too. Most self-respecting students spoke a common language of cynicism and in my case it flowed from deep inside.

The Christians' pleasantness always unsettled me and sometimes it threw me totally. One day I was sitting in the canteen at college. I'd just bought a see-through dress in a King's Road fashion boutique and thought I looked great in it. I waved a foul, but indispensable Gauloise, while displaying to perfection my fingernails, each carefully painted a different colour. Long, dark hair hung over my pale face like a curtain, but I flicked it to one side when my eyes sought and made contact with his. He was a horn player from the brass section of First Orchestra. I could do worse. At least brass players were known for a certain level of cool. Or as much as any music student could hope to attain, I thought gloomily! Still, something was happening between us, that wonderful, magical, all-beguiling stirring of mutual attraction. It was just a matter of time....

And then they arrived—the happy band of pilgrims, all Jesus stickers and bright smiles. Bearing the token cup of coffee bravely before them, they annihilated my image in seconds. I could only watch as my horn player stubbed out his fag and fled from the canteen, without bothering to disguise his horror.

Cherith in particular remained remorselessly nice to me and I had to take care. Her sister was nearly engaged to a man from my dad's church. Too close...too nice! I protected myself by attacking her. Singers were fair game. Unlike 'proper' musicians they held most of their practice sessions while walking around the college. I could usually hear Cherith coming. Upon noticing me, she would interrupt her vocal exercise or Mozart aria with a cheery greeting. Utterly uninhibited, utterly unaffected—why didn't she just leave me alone?

But soon the Christians became the least of my worries. Anna would not answer the phone. I hadn't seen her for nearly a week. Her flat-mate explained that Anna felt so mixed up emotionally that she had visited a doctor. He had told her to keep away from stress of any kind, and that, it seemed, included me. It took a while for the words to sink in. I just could not come to terms with the situation.

By this time my brother had married and moved to Bristol. Devastated, I retreated down there for a few days and poured out my desperation in poetry:

> Though I live a thousand years,
> And walk upon a thousand streets,
> I know I will not find a place
> Wherein I do not see your face.

> This pain is more than I can bear
> Without your love, without you there,
> And, even as it fades a while,
> A person smiles, I see your smile.

> I learn to face the pain of night
> I almost see the break of day
> And then, as if I have no choice,
> A person speaks, I hear your voice.

Back in London I took more drugs in an attempt to cushion the pain. Then, not long after Anna walked out of my life, I noticed THE American. I was not stoned enough to be immune to him, he wore the kind of clothes which everyone wanted. No way could you buy denims that good in England in 1970. He noticed me and we made eye contact, but his words hardly came as the chat-up line I had been expecting.

'You remind me of someone,' he said. I wondered which exotic actress he would name, but a look of concern crossed his face as he explained, 'It's my sister. She started doing dope a couple years back.'

Was it that obvious, I wondered? The American talked about how his sister had slid into a real mess, 'And you're fast going the same way!'

Our eyes locked. For one moment we hovered on the brink of seriousness, then my mind came down like a shutter, as I distanced myself yet again through my old defence system of cynicism and contempt. What a shame! He had promised more. Who would have believed that *he* would lecture me, almost like my parents? Yet his out-of-the-blue warning came only six weeks before the bad drug trip at St Margaret's Bay brought my life to a crisis point and everything changed.

In fact, most people with any sense of perception at all at that time must have seen me as a wreck— only, being English, they never said so. I viewed myself quite differently—as an *avant-garde* person, talented, but not given to taking work too seriously. I knew how to look after myself and get just what I wanted. I took great care to wear absurdly fashionable clothes and the right expression, but kept my emotions in the deep freeze. Nothing could touch me. I had even partially silenced the old 'Who am I?' question which haunted me. My image said it all.

The bad trip on LSD demolished many of my cherished illusions. I felt myself teetering on the edge of an abyss, out of control and taken over by fear. Clothes and talent gave scant protection. With my image under threat I plunged into a sort of nothingness, and if I allowed myself to think about the future I sensed only fear, chaos and disaster.

It is possible that without the prayers of my parents and of people like Cherith I would have died during some LSD extravaganza. I had several near-misses. But Cherith had been praying for me, and despite all the barriers I put up she never doubted that God's Spirit would reach through to me, one day. Perhaps then it is not so surprising, when the chips were down and I realised I had to find help, that I turned like a homing pigeon to Christians, and to all I had learnt as a child. I thought I'd burnt my bridges too thoroughly for any return. Fortunately, Christians at the Royal College had taken the trouble to make themselves known. I knew instinctively that they had constructed a new bridge so that I could reach them—and maybe even reach God—if I wanted.

When I whispered down the phone to Cherith, 'I'm in a mess!', she jumped in her car and hurtled across London to find me. Despite my new-found vulnerability I only had to look at her to know that there was hope for me—and a way out. I didn't have to leap off the cliff of nothingness and despair after all. I had somewhere to go with people who would welcome and help me. The admission that I needed help had been the hardest part.

When Cherith took me back to her home, Christians came crawling out of the woodwork, including specimens of the most conventional men I had seen in my entire life. Talk about uncool—cheap suits, short hair…every ounce of my flesh reeled backwards. What had I done? Would I mutate into the prototype splodge-Christian? Even if it never came to that I knew the score. I would have to give up smoking, drinking and sex, and, worst of all…go to church.

For two days a battle raged inside me. If this was the answer did I really want to know? If only I could find another solution! During this traumatic time I learned that Dad was staying with an aunt in another part of London—which I found surprising because he rarely left his responsibilities in Sidmouth. When I phoned him he understood from my confused ramblings that I might be on the verge of becoming a Christian and careered across south London to meet me. With my dad, in Cherith's mum's lounge, I knelt down and gave my life to Jesus. Even as I prayed I knew that something dramatic had happened, but how do you describe uttering a prayer feeling lost and alone in an empty universe and coming out of it, a minute later, knowing that the whole cosmos is full of someone who loves you?

I got up and gave everyone a hug, including the men who had seemed so wet. So much for my cynicism! These Christians no longer seemed revolting but almost normal, and I marvelled at the extent to which my prejudice had distorted my vision. Somehow I knew that God had broken down some kind of wall which I had built inside myself. I felt that I could belong here and I felt good.

An overjoyed Dad spoke of how much he and Mum had worried about me. They had prayed regularly, but Mum had always felt fearful until one day the Lord caught her attention, saying that he loved me even more than she did and that she must place me in his hands. Now, just a few weeks after she had let go of the responsibility and handed it over to God, I had become a Christian.

I still needed help. Peggy, Cherith's Mum, had been staying in Ireland and, as we drove to meet her at the airport, I knew that I still felt vulnerable. I found it desperately important that this stranger should show kindness to me. She did—beyond anything I could have hoped for. Her husband was dying of Parkinson's disease and she had four grown-up children still at home, yet she took me in as well. In fact, she became like a spiritual mother to me. I loved the Millburn-Fryer's house with its spacious rooms. One even contained two upright pianos. Cherith and I had great fun playing duets on them.

Those first months as a Christian were magical. 'The Lord'—as I now knew him and called him—met me in a dramatic way and appeared to deal with all the terrors brought on by LSD. I felt safe, accepted and loved, and I spent many hours with my new family of Christians, learning to open up to them. Of course, I soon found out that none of them was perfect, they all had their little idiosyncrasies and selfish moments. On the whole, though, I found their lack of hardness and cynicism refreshing. Most of them, being arts students, were also creative—the best of both worlds.

6

Private Lives: Public Faces

> Last night I dreamt that you were there,
> I felt your warmth, I felt your care,
> Forbidden echoes rose to energise my heart,
> But as I went to call your name
> I realised you'd gone again
> And I awoke to find a cold and empty night.

I had been living in a dark room all of my days, aware that sometimes I tripped over obstacles which hurt me, though I had no idea what they were or how to move them out of the way. When I met Jesus the light switched on, and for the first couple of months I staggered round my world, punch-drunk, exclaiming, 'Ooh, that's nice! Ooh, so's that!' I would stare in wonder at the light, dazzled by its brilliance, then rush out to tell my friends, 'Come and see! Look, I have electricity now!' I wanted them to ask Jesus to turn on their light too.

All the teaching which I had received as a child came bobbing to the surface of my life, like so many corks which had been trapped at the bottom of a pond. I knew, without being told, that I should read the Bible and pray. These things no longer seemed boring and meaningless, they came alive with dynamic relevance.

It was a good time to become a Christian. The wind of the Holy Spirit had just begun to blow again through some churches. He brought new life through organisations like the Fountain Trust and through people such as Jean Darnall. Whenever we could we went to meetings to find out more—especially to a place called Post Green near Poole in Dorset. A couple called Sir Tom and Lady Faith Lees owned a large house and grounds there, which they threw open for Christian camps at Easter and in the summer. At the camps they held meetings quite unlike the boring church services I remembered. In a super-charged atmosphere everything came alive with colour, freedom, movement and laughter. God was speaking to people and changing them—you could see it!

Lots of things happened to me at Post Green. First I noticed, to my surprise, that the teenage girls from the Lees family wore Laura Ashley clothes—the pinnacle of fashion then. Prior to that I had decided, after a struggle, that I needed to conform to the Christian look, so I'd bought some nice frilly frocks in C&A. They really did not suit my personality, so it came as a huge relief when I saw that God had never wanted my old image replaced with compulsory prettiness. Instead he aimed to change my whole outlook on life. Considering it had landed me in such a mess, that did not seem so very hard. Back home, I sorted through my wardrobe. Clearly some see-through clothes would have to go, but the Lord seemed happy with several of my old favourites.

Also at Post Green I came to a place of real sorrow

and repentance over the way in which I had lived and treated people in the past. Some people say that you cannot become a Christian without true repentance—a full turning away from selfish desires to follow his way—but I know that I met God before that happened. Of course I had said 'sorry' in a casual kind of way when I first prayed at Cherith's, but I came to Jesus on the basis of my need. Self-centred as ever, I wanted him to get me out of a mess, to use him just as I used everyone else. I suppose I did repent in the sense that I was willing for him to change me, but I don't think I realised how awful sin and selfishness were, because, like many of my generation, I had lived in an amoral rather than an immoral way. In my arrogance I had restructured morality to suit myself and ended by having none. That explained why the Christian moral absolutes used to infuriate me so.

Now I became more and more aware of who God really was. This meant I became overwhelmed by his incredible undeserved favour in accepting me, despite the selfish way in which I had come to him. What a grotesque parody my self-centred ways had made of the person God had created me to be! As the light of a holy God showed up my filthiness I began to weep from a very deep place. And then I cried even more as he showed me how much it had cost him to deal with sin through the Cross, taking my punishment himself so that now I could be forgiven and even be his friend.

As we were singing and worshipping God on one occasion I began to feel a weird sensation, a dreadful churning like rats in my stomach. I sensed that something was trying to pull me out of the meeting and out of the whole camp. A man came over and asked me what was the matter. 'How should I know? I've never felt like this before!' I snapped, panicking. He fetched Sir Tom and Lady Faith. They asked if I had ever had any involvement with occult cere-monies and I remembered some of the things we had done at Dartington College. They prayed calmly, releasing me in the name of Jesus and at once I felt something leave me, something oppressive which lifted from me in a very definite way. As the weeks went by I noticed a new lightness and freedom in all sorts of everyday situations.

Soon I sensed the power of God being poured into me. I later found that this was called the baptism of the Holy Spirit. I spoke in a special language given to me by God. Because I had never learnt this language I expected Jean Darnall to swoop down at any min-ute and pronounce that I was making it all up. But I felt incredibly close to God. I knew, really *knew*, he loved me. And I found this new means of expression, this 'gift of tongues' helpful in expressing all I felt to God, day by day. My grounding as a new Christian not only included experiences like this but also plenty of teaching about how better to follow Jesus.

I decided that, in order to show that I was serious about going on with God, I would ask my father to baptise me. I felt so encouraged when a girl I knew, called Linda Smith, who worked as a chambermaid in a Sidmouth hotel, became a Christian during my baptism service! Though she had not seemed to make much of her life up to then, afterwards she enrolled on a teaching course at Southlands College, where she became President of the Christian Union and later went on to become a highly-respected college lecturer.

Back in London, somewhere in the bowels of Battersea, I found an Anglican church which, like Post Green, was moving in the realms of the Spirit. Pete Phillip worked as curate there and I became friends with him and his wife Beth. They knew the flamboyant American Arthur Blessit, who literally carried a huge wooden cross round the world to draw people's attention to his gospel message. Arthur was about to tour a few venues around London and had asked the Phillips to find a band to sing at these events. The church organist, a young architect called Keith Routledge, turned out to be a brilliant jazz pianist. Angie, his wife, sang. I met them and some of their musical friends—a drummer, bass player and more singers—at the Phillips' and we formed the band Meet Jesus Music. I was one of the lead singers and we spent many enjoyable hours preparing material for Arthur's tour.

Crowds packed into Westminster Central Hall, the Empire Pool, Wembley, and the famous church of All Souls, Langham Place. We sang, and then Arthur spoke about how people could come to know Jesus as their own Lord and friend. Many people met Jesus for the first time at those meetings. I thought it was wonderful. I loved to see others find the best thing that had ever happened to me—to find Jesus, who was making such a difference in my life. After all the things I had gone through, I had quite a story and was only too happy to tell it—in public, on a one-to-one basis after the concerts, around College, anywhere...This delighted the rest of the group.

'What a find—Lou's not only musical but real living evidence that Jesus can do spectacular things.'

When the Arthur Blessit tour came to an end it seemed a shame that the group should split up. The Lord appeared to have put us together and he certainly used us to good effect. Meet Jesus Music became increasingly well known as we reached out to people in gigs laid on by various local groups of Christians all over the country. We often worked with a young evangelist called Eric Delve, who has since developed a much wider and better known ministry.

Back in the early '70s, Christians had begun to realise that music could serve as an excellent medium for communicating the good news about Jesus. However, three chords cheerfully strummed on a guitar, while someone kind of sang along more or less in tune, hardly conveyed the right kind of message. A more professional approach would do no harm. We aimed for high standards as a group, both in the way we presented ourselves and musically. We often used close three-part harmony, but styles varied according to who wrote the piece. Keith preferred smoochy, laid-back jazz, Dave liked the country and western style, while my songs (which came later) could best be described as lyrical rock. We were all pretty versatile in both style and the number of instruments we could play, and people said that our work had an innovative quality.

Touring had its lighter moments too. In the middle of one song, Tony used to perform a brilliant drum solo which lasted several minutes. He would build it up, then bring the volume right down until the singers and other instruments came back in. But, at the Empire Pool, Wembley, the man who had introduced us stepped in just before the drum solo ended, saying, 'Well, thank you very much, Meet Jesus Music!' as we valiantly choked back half-formed notes. Another time we were not received quite as we expected in a Calvinistic Baptist church. A man actually stood up and interrupted Tony, in mid-drumming. 'I think we should stop all this nasty satanic music now, don't you?' he spluttered. Poor Tony, such a tender-hearted man, felt dreadful.

He is a pastor now. (In fact, of the seven of us, several are in full-time Christian work. Others have backed down on their Christian commitment altogether, which really saddens me, as they seemed so strong at the time and all helped me so much.)

So here I was, less than a year since my bad trip on LSD, standing out in front, being used by God, with all my problems solved having found at last who I was meant to be! Little did I know what lay round the corner, or how dramatically it would bring to an end this honeymoon period of my Christian life.

In the summer just before my third and final year at the Royal College Anna got over her troubles, whatever they were, and came to find me in Sidmouth. The moment I saw her again I knew that I still loved her very deeply. None of the feelings had changed, and yet our relationship could hardly continue as before. Part of the trouble lay in the fact that I had never given her up, though she had abandoned me for a time. Anna knew that I still loved her, that she still had a magnetic hold on me. I could not seem to summon up the strength to resist her and we ended up in bed together. Afterwards I felt dreadful, torn between the two loves of my life. My sanity, my very being depended on God. I had been in such a mess without him that I could not afford to go back on my Christian commitment, even had I wanted to. By this time I knew Jesus well enough to love him deeply. It hurt me when I hurt him.

I realised that this sin, like any other, had nothing to do with breaking the spoil-sport rules of some dictator-God. The Bible's prohibitions always had good reasons behind them. God made me and he knew me. Outside of marriage, sex—whether lesbian or heterosexual—did not offend him more than any other sin, but it did have greater potential than most for harm. I knew that if I continued with this affair it would destroy me and probably Anna as well. It would affect the Christians I loved and confuse many who had recently found my Lord through Meet Jesus Music. Yet still I could not break free from Anna.

'Dear Lord, let her become a Christian!' I prayed that so many times, with all of my heart. She had no church contacts, so far as I knew. Of course, God must have sent her back into my life so that I could help her to find Jesus for herself! I decided to take her to some meetings. Because of her love of intellectual things I took her to the L'Abri Centre in Ealing. Originally founded by the Christian philosopher, Francis Schaeffer, the L'Abri Centres geared their teaching especially to appeal to students. Anna went along willingly enough since it meant spending time with me. She would sit through the talks with one corner of her mouth turned down in a sardonic expression. I knew that she found the Christian message quite ridiculous—but then so had I. However, I failed to realise that she had every reason not to embrace Christianity, since its teaching clearly forbade our lesbian relationship which had become of all-consuming importance to her once more.

When L'Abri offered communion one day, Anna behaved in a very strange way. She seemed almost to froth at the mouth. Had I been more knowledgeable about demonic activity in those days, I might have known what to do. As things stood I saw only tremendous anger, and never dared ask her to a church meeting again.

I kept my Christian friends pretty much in the dark about my struggles over this relationship, because I felt such deep shame. As for Anna, if ever she met them she would express her scorn subtly, through clever, sardonic humour.

By this time I was sharing a bed-sit with Linda Smith, the girl who had become a Christian at my baptism. (Two Lindas in such a small space became confusing—so my Dartington nickname of Lindy-Lou became plain Lou, which has stuck ever since.) I would never meet Anna at the flat of course. We usually chose neutral ground, but she turned up sometimes at the Royal College. Once she made a scene there, blocking the doorway and refusing to let me out until we had talked. A growing sense of unease began to gnaw at me, trapping me into facing the fact that Anna's behaviour was becoming increasingly obsessive. At one time my need of her had fed our relationship. Now my fear of her, or of the way she behaved, was becoming stronger than my need.

I was alone at the bed-sit one night when Anna arrived unexpectedly. We began to get physical when suddenly I pulled away, shouting, 'No!' and repeated for the umpteenth time that we could no longer be lovers. Sensing perhaps that I meant it this time, she began to shake me in sheer frustration. It hurt. I struggled, then started to panic as I realised that she had her hands on my neck so tight that no air could reach my windpipe. In her fit of blind rage she probably had no idea that she was strangling me.

At that moment I heard a key turn in the lock and Linda walked in. She managed to pull Anna off me and Linda and I ran straight out of the open door, racing to a Christian family who lived just down the road. When we returned to the flat Anna had gone, but later we discovered holes in a large, family-style Bible which my father had given me. We examined it and found that it had been pierced from the front cover right through to Paul's epistles. The only implement in the bed-sit which fitted the gashes turned out to be a letter opener in the shape of a dagger. We had no conclusive proof that Anna had done this—but who else? Linda's boyfriend remarked, 'She's got some strength there!' He picked up the flimsy paper opener and gave it a good try himself, but though he struck with all his strength the dagger penetrated the Bible barely as far as Isaiah.

He and Linda were worried. 'This is getting beyond a joke. You must inform College, Lou.' I had to agree, and the next day I told my tutor what had happened. She advised me to leave London for a couple of weeks until the heat had died down.

7
Demolition Job

Stop! I'm trying to save you.
Wait, I'm trying to heal you.
Listen, I'm trying to set you free;
Stop building walls around your life.

You've got a well-conducted, well constructed blue-
    print to survive,
A carefully cultivated social smile that never reached
    your eyes—
But I know you!
I want to bring you alive.

I went to stay in Buckinghamshire at the head-
quarters of a missionary organisation called WEC,
where a lovely couple called Len and Iris Moules
took an interest in me. They helped a good deal and
it made a wonderful break. I even gave up smoking
while I stayed with them and did not touch another
cigarette for a considerable number of years.

Unfortunately, I could not stay at WEC forever. I
had to get back to College and I needed a home in
London which would give me some kind of protection from Anna. I found it in the shape of an old

69

Latvian lady with the unlikely-sounding name of Miss Kavistick. Miss K, as we called her, was one of the strongest people I have ever met—strong in faith and will, that is. Having tackled all sorts of things in the past, including running a mental hospital, it was nothing to her to organise with military precision everyone who lived at the Pye Barn Trust Refuge for People in Need. Yet I found when I had moved in that she also had a heart of gold.

Life at Miss K's proved anything but dull. She had enormous character and a blithe disregard for the subtleties of life. Once, when Jehovah's Witnesses called at the door, she invited them to supper. This gave her the chance to say grace. 'Dear Lord,' she began in her precise, accented tones, 'we thank you for the Trinity—for Father, Son and Holy Spirit!' Not the most subtle way to start a red hot debate about the divinity of Jesus and the Holy Spirit, but effective!

The house had been acquired cheaply because of a sitting tenant, who would sometimes appear at meals, inevitably when we had company, and shuffle round carrying a pot full of urine, chanting, 'I don't know what to do with it! I don't know what to do with it!' We realised that she was developing dementia, but her behaviour seemed no more bizarre than that of some of the other residents. For example, one woman regularly wandered down the garden in the middle of the night warbling songs from *The Sound of Music*.

The indomitable Miss K shepherded us all to any Christian meetings she thought might do us good, and sometimes invited stray Christians back to the house. She introduced me to one—a trumpeter from the Marine Music Corps and said that she thought I should accompany him on the piano. Only at that point did he realise that she expected him to give a concert in the house that evening. The look of surprise on his face made it worth my being bossed around. But dear Miss K in the end proved very good for me. Though we often clashed, she prayed, bullied and encouraged me through many traumas. I am extremely grateful to her and love her dearly. We still write to one another, though she is over seventy now. Her letters tend to arrive in bulk, five at a time in a single envelope, because she forgot to post the earlier ones!

Meanwhile Anna spent a few months in the States, where perhaps she realised that there was life after Lou. She contacted me on her return and I sensed that her need for me was no longer so obsessive. She seemed truly sorry for the way she had behaved. I still saw her from time to time, when my need for her grew stronger than my fear of her violence. I think she realised that another scene would cause me to back off completely. She may even have sensed that she was losing me, because her visits had become too traumatic to handle.

I felt torn in two, still sleeping with her sometimes, still hoping against hope that she would become a Christian and that we would be able to express our love in a valid way. Maybe one day it would all work out. Eventually I felt so mixed up that I decided to talk the whole affair through with Keith Routledge, the leader of Meet Jesus Music. 'To be honest Lou, I think there's only one way, and that's never to see her again.' Keith paused and looked at me, worry lines creasing his face. He knew how much this would cost and feared which way I might jump. 'I don't believe it's just me saying that, Lou. I believe it's from the Lord.' I forced my eyes to look directly at his. 'I know it is, Keith.'

I saw Anna one more time after that. We sat behind the television in the Common Room one afternoon at College and held hands. I told her I couldn't see her again. Though I had said the words before, this time was different. Anna knew that I meant it and chose to let me go. She walked out of the room. I have not set eyes on her since.

Feeling utterly bereft I returned to Miss Kavistick's that evening. Over the next months the old lady helped me more than I can say. I could talk anything out with her because nothing shocked her or destroyed her deep well of unconditional love. It takes commitment to hang onto a vision when all you can see is problems, but like Cherith, Miss K was one of those people who communicated specific faith. I knew she never doubted my potential, never doubted God would see me through—and that gave me strength to go on.

A few hours after I had said goodbye to Anna I had the scary sensation that she was calling to me across London. Miss K prayed with tremendous authority in the name of Jesus that Anna and I be cut off from one another. That was when I felt the break—when I really knew that the spiritual tie had been broken and that our relationship had truly ended.

It didn't stop my grief, however. Much later I read Anna's name whilst glancing at the credits on a well-known record and my heart nearly stopped. It hurt, leaving her. It hurt for years afterwards. Lesbian relationships are often intense and deep with complex roots and complex reasons why they began in the first place although I didn't realise that at the time. No one around me then had the capacity to help me consider what had driven me, let alone to help me find a solution to those root problems. So I found the sudden break almost unbearable.

I knew that being in love with another woman was wrong. So was expressing that love sexually. On the other hand, a part of my love for Anna was valid and beautiful, and I had to let that go along with the rest. So much for God sorting out all my problems. Now I had a whole new set and most days I hardly knew how to struggle on.

All this time I had been out there in the spotlight with Meet Jesus Music, singing about the good news of Jesus, and God in his mercy still used me to help all sorts of people. But I hated the hypocrisy, the widening crevasse between where I stood and where I knew I should be. Every time I had weakened and returned to Anna guilt gnawed at me, and despite picking myself up and going back to God and the group, I felt so vulnerable. I know now that others, in far more exalted positions than myself, can experience marathon struggles of a similar nature. At the time I felt simply devastated that my wonderful new relationship with this amazing God had soured through the guilt and shame which I had brought upon myself.

But God had started a different kind of work on me, stirring around deep in my life, exposing many things I had not wanted to see. At first Jesus had poured out his blessing on me in a painless rescue operation—painless for me, though not for him. At first I had gazed, overjoyed, at God's dazzling brilliance, but now it spotlighted the dirt in my life. 'Dear, Lord,' I prayed, 'you don't stock dimmer switches, do you?'

Since becoming a Christian I had not felt again the terrible fear which had gripped me after my drugs trip. I had a few flashbacks, where colours began to drip into one another, but these soon passed. Then, one weekend shortly after my baptism and after I had renewed my relationship with Anna, I travelled to stay with a friend in Nottingham. Suddenly the world around me seemed remote. I could hear my heart thundering inside. Unease grew until I knew only an icy fear, made somehow more terrible because no hallucinations flashed me back to past experiences. I phoned my parents in desperation. Kind as ever, they responded to my tears by driving all the way north from Sidmouth, and then took me back to London.

A few weeks later I was travelling to College one morning on the Northern Line when the tube train shuddered to a halt in a dark tunnel near Kennington. It often stuck at that particular spot. On this occasion though I started to panic, really panic. My own fear scared me so much that I vowed never to risk triggering it by using the tube again. I switched to buses, reasoning that if God had wanted me to travel in holes he would have made me a mole. My solution seemed simple. But then I had another panic attack in the pedestrian tunnel between Imperial College and South Kensington. Soon I felt uncomfortable in many situations outside my own home. A pressing need to avoid them took over my life.

During this period, when I prayed for people after concerts I felt good, though my personal life slid ever faster into a mess until negative emotions became overpowering. My parents called in Arthur Wallis, a well-known Christian speaker, to pray because I had struck a real depression. I failed to improve. After the final parting from Anna I found myself still more deeply depressed and almost housebound. I had agoraphobia.

I know now that the best thing I could have done after the initial incident in the tube was to face it again immediately—a bit like getting back on a horse straight after falling off. But I believe that being stuck in a dark tunnel merely triggered my terror. It flowed out of wells of loneliness and even deeper problems, which had been released to flood through me by the painful separation from Anna. I had hardly known fear as a teenager. Like other emotions I had built walls against it since my child-hood, though it had surfaced in a devastating way through LSD. Then God had seemed to put my life straight. But now everything seemed changed.

'I cannot conceive a day, Lord, when I will ever be free from fear,' I wrote in my diary. 'Terror has become so much part of my life that you name it and I'm frightened of it! Frightened to go out, frightened to stay in, frightened of crowds, frightened to be alone.' This was only the beginning of a long period dominated by assorted phobias and depression. I waded through thick blackness every day, fighting to achieve the simplest of things.

Even practising my instrument for College had become a nightmare. Since I had shared such a deep love of music with Anna, I could hardly cope with the feelings it aroused in me. Luckily I could choose when to take my lessons at College. I crammed them all into Tuesdays and Thursdays and worked out the location of various vicarages and churches on the route between Miss K's and College. At least I could dive into one of these safe places if a panic attack overcame me. And so I tottered from one to another, like a tiny child lurching between pieces of furniture. I spent the weekends dreading Tuesdays. Fridays seemed the bright spot of my week, with three clear days before I needed to venture out. Being house-bound, at least I did more work—which must explain how I managed to obtain my degree!

All this time I continued to sing with Meet Jesus Music. They delivered me door-to-door, to and from concerts. Sometimes the sheer noise of our gigs would trigger flash-backs to my bad trip. I found the long drum solo especially difficult in this respect and I only managed to appear at all because of the support the group gave me. After concerts I still talked to individuals, still led them to Jesus—not difficult when I switched on my 'Spiritual Gospel Singer' persona. To be fair, as I had become a Christian so recently the experience still lived for me and I genu-inely longed for more people to know Jesus. Though totally out of my depth, I even managed what I called 'counselling', which really meant giving 'coin-in-the-slot' responses. Sermons and books explained that the answer to A lay in B and C, so if someone had a problem, I had a verse for it. Sharing formula scriptures did not require me to engage in any real compassion or kindness. Sharing my true self never occurred to me because, once again, I had lost any sense of who I was.

Meet Jesus Music had a number called 'Where Jesus Is'. Everything you need can be found in him we sang—love, joy, happiness, freedom, peace of mind. Lovely song, but oh, what irony. If the audience had only known! The credibility gap between my words on stage and the real state of my life widened by the hour. Yet strangely, in the midst of hurricane-like emotions, sometimes I found an eye of peace in Jesus. After the bad trip on LSD I knew that if fear continued in such intensity it would send me insane. But now I could turn to Jesus—and turn to him I did in my desperation. If nothing else, those dark months forced my roots deeper into God, and sometimes I experienced a powerful sense of his presence with me. I felt a real sense of achievement, merely for having survived a day—and I knew I only did that because the Lord had helped me through. Certainly I could no longer afford to mess around as a Christian; I needed to get down to serious business with God.

Desperate for anything which would feed my faith and drown out my inner well of pessimism, I found some records by an American group called Second Chapter of Acts. They not only played superb music, but Annie Herring's words came from her heart. Unusually for those days, when most Christian music concentrated on a simple evangelistic message, Annie sang of her relationship with God. I sensed tht she had been through some dark places, but that God had pulled her through. Her songs often gave me the courage to open my front door in the morning.

Some of Jamie Owen's tracks spoke of God's grace

and they also reached a deep place within me, especially one song, called 'Hard Times Make You Strong'. Mere words of comfort, even from the Bible, tended to go in one ear and out the other, but music like this filtered through to steady and bathe me in the unconditional love of Jesus.

Many evenings I spent kneeling beside my bed, crying my eyes out. 'I don't understand what I'm going through, Lord! I'm tired of asking why and tired of begging you to take away my fear.' Then, one time, I added, 'If I must go through this, all I ask is that you give me music—music which will help other people. That at least would make some sense of the pain, Lord.' One evening, when praying, I wandered up to the piano in my bedroom and found myself playing a melody. Soon I had written the song, 'I am the Way'. Naively I pitched it in too high a key to sing myself, but that was good news for people like Dave Pope and Marilyn Baker who used it! Soon a couple called Dave and Dana sang some more songs which I had just written.

I found it hard to transpose properly, so never sung some of my songs myself. Others I began to sing haltingly to my friends. One day Keith suggested I tried one in a concert. Heart pounding, hands shaking, I gave my first public performance of my own work. After that Meet Jesus Music gave me a regular slot and I began to develop more of my own material. My songs had credibility because the songs were me!

> In the midst of a noisy city
> I need you here beside me Lord,
> In a place with no peace or pity
> I need you here beside me Lord.

At College I felt moderately safe. People there had a liberal outlook. But life became harder after my Finals when the familiar structure of my week disappeared. I stayed on in London, not only because of Meet Jesus Music, but because I knew that the answer to my problems did not lie in running away. I found a series of jobs to support myself. What a nightmare! One involved peripatetic (travelling) music teaching of all things. I taught part-time in a school for maladjusted boys and part-time in a primary school in Lambeth. At one stage I gave private piano lessons to a pupil who lived off the King's Road.

On journeys to all these places I coped in two ways. I had come across a book which told the true story of someone whose problems seemed nearly as bad as my own. Though she suffered a long time in the end she had found a way through. She gave me hope and I carried that book with me everywhere. I also prayed in tongues a good deal, muttering frantically under my breath. I used to wonder whatever people must think of me and then one day a parent at one of the schools made a comment which knocked me backwards. 'You always look so peaceful, Miss Hayles.' *Peaceful* was hardly the word I would have chosen to describe the way my heart curled and thumped! I had perceived my life as a grim struggle for a long, long time though in my saner moments I knew that only the Lord kept me together at all.

At one point, some bright spark at the school for maladjusted boys decided that breeding spiders would make a wonderfully educational project. Now, I am terrified of spiders, but if any of the boys had found *that* out my life in the school would have become impossible. So whenever a boy approached me with a huge specimen and asked me to examine the hairs on its legs, I had to find strength to pretend a vital interest. And, since my own mental resources had been exhausted in overcoming my fears of travelling that morning, only Jesus could supply the shortfall.

Then the head teacher had the scintillating idea of asking me to organise a music concert. This challenge drove me to fervent prayer since I had a good idea what would happen—and it did. On the day every child acted like a prima donna. One boy insisted on performing the whole of his solo whilst hiding behind the piano. Another stopped in mid-recorder ensemble, stammered, 'I knew I'd go wrong, miss!' and stormed off stage. Nevertheless the parents so appreciated the concert that the head asked me to do one every term. How I wished that God had failed to answer my prayers for success!

The head was intrigued by my Christian faith and asked me to take an assembly. I knew those lads and how they were likely to respond. More fervent prayer ascended to heaven. 'I'm not going to talk about religion,' I said, 'because you'd be bored rigid. But if I brought in a man who could walk across the swimming pool and turn water into wine, I think you'd be really fascinated. Jesus did those things and much, much more. Christianity is being introduced to Jesus and experiencing him personally.'

Afterwards an Irish teacher came up to me in the staff room and asked the perfect question, 'How can I experience God personally?' I was very happy to tell her. Only later did I learn that in fact she came from an order of nuns whose vocation involved working incognito in secular settings. My simple words to those boys had cut through years of her religious striving to reach God, enabling me to point out that he had already built a bridge to reach her.

Maybe God's light did shine through my gloom to help others, but my fears still had consequences. I started a Christian Union in the school, and of the three or four boys who came along David really wanted to know God the most. He had become a Christian at a summer camp. I read his case history—how he had been born in a mental hospital to a heroin addict and how he had never known a consistent mother-figure in his life. My heart went out to him and I decided that, as the only committed Christian in the school, perhaps I could become a kind of replacement mother to him. Our relationship deepened and I promised myself that I would never let him down. Then one day he phoned me, obviously distressed. He wanted me to meet him in a part of Notting Hill which I did not know. I had not been honest with David about my agoraphobia. I had thought that if he found out about my struggles, it might destroy his embryonic faith. So I could not tell him that my fear prevented me from meeting him right then and there. I made some feeble excuse. He insisted that it was really important that I go. I refused and our relationship was never the same again.

We both went our separate ways when he left school shortly afterwards. I managed to put him in touch with some other Christians, who tried to reach out to him, but later I heard that he committed suicide by putting a shot-gun to his head. David suffered dreadful mental anguish all his short life and

I am sure that God in his mercy took him to himself. The tragedy is that if I came across another David today I feel I would be able to help him find healing, or I would know of others who could. But the Lord spoke to me that day I could not be there for David, and his words have remained with me ever since. 'You cannot be God to anyone. You can never meet all their needs.'

8

Christians in Hobnailed Boots

Sometimes I feel so shaken that my very roots are
    breaking up
Everyone seems to be leaning on me, but I feel so
    alone.
Lord, you know my feet are falling
But my weary voice is calling you.
Your arms are everlasting, will you carry me home?

Put my feet on the Rock for everything else is sinking
    sand.
Put my feet on the Rock, for heaven and earth will
    fade away,
But the Rock will stand.

I once taught two sisters to play the piano. Rachel, a
confident achiever, needed goals. If I gave her a
piece two grades beyond her standard, she would rise
to the challenge and make great strides forward.
Sensitive Becky, on the other hand, felt far less sure
of herself. If she had trouble handling even one bar in
a piece she would worry so much that she made little
progress during the week. I learned that I had to
treat the two sisters very differently if each were to
achieve her musical potential.

During the period when I struggled with life in London I identified more with the Beckies of this world. Ordinary things, which once I would have found easy, now took all my willpower. Hearty challenges scared me rigid. Going along to a meeting was a major achievement in its own right. Out of a sense of faithfulness I sat tight all the way through it, despite waves of claustrophobia and sheer panic. I must have looked unresponsive and miserable—anything but spiritual. Only God knew how much it cost me to stay there. I don't think many of my Christian friends understood what was going on. Looking back on that time, I am grateful for one thing, though. It reminds me not to judge other people by appearances.

With all my energies focused on remaining in the building I was in no fit state to receive anything from a service or from Christian teaching, let alone able to rise to any of the challenges issued. I could no more have taken the Gospel to other nations than flown to Mars without a rocket! Of course, the many Rachels in the meeting needed to be provoked, stretched and challenged, but I do believe the church must realise that everyone is different—or at different stages.

Sometimes I was afraid that I was developing a chip on my shoulder as a result of experiences I had been through, but I have seen so many other people plunged into a pit of despair by a rousing sermon that I wonder where some Christian ministry leaves people who are hurting. The more I talk with those people, the more I realise that many of them have justification for their grievances. An army encouraged to march in hobnailed boots must take care not to trample its own battle-wounded underfoot, for

Jesus says, 'A bruised reed I will not break.' He carries the poor and the broken on his back and remains the friend of sinners.

Of course I knew that God didn't want my life dominated by fear. Desperate for my problems to disappear, I leapt forward if anyone hinted they might pray about anything remotely connected with them. Gullible and vulnerable, I would have crawled through a drainpipe in the name of Jesus ten times, if someone had told me it would help. Many people did pray for me. They prayed against my fear, or my depression, or both. I lost count of the number of times someone rebuked or cast out a 'spirit of fear' from me. That was it, as far as they were concerned—Lou had been set free, just like in the Bible when Jesus cast evil spirits out of people. Whatever you prayed in Jesus' name, if it was God's will, it happened. There could be no doubt of God's will in this case. The Bible says that God has not given us a spirit of fear, but of love, power and a sound mind. Well, there you go Lou, rejoice girl, you're set free and isn't Jesus wonderful?

But as I turned to leave the hall, trying to believe this time that the deliverance from fear had worked, agoraphobia enveloped me in its choking cloud. I'd stumble on, straining to believe that it would clear, rebuking the fear in Jesus' name, calling it a lie. The Bible says that God has a spiritual enemy, a being called Satan. He (or his minions) were merely trying to fool me into believing that he had won, so I kept declaring out loud that I had been set free. But after a few days I could no longer deny the reality. I would have to admit that nothing had changed. Well-known ministers prayed with me sometimes, real men of God. I could find no fault with their splendid credentials of faith, so any blockage must lie within myself, I reasoned.

'God does not want you to be frightened,' they said to me. In my state of mind I took this as a rebuke. God must be displeased because fear still ruled me. But it came nowhere near the abyss of horror which I had experienced during the bad drug trip—and only God had rescued me from that. So I could not even run away from this angry God. I had no safe place to go.

After prayer and 'deliverance' inevitably I felt worse than before. I entered meetings with one problem—acute phobia—and often left with three, feeling a total failure and unworthy of God. Could a person reach a place beyond salvation, I wondered? It certainly seemed that way. My friends spent hours talking to me. 'Think of the 365 "Fear nots" in the Bible, Lou, one for every day of the year. Claim them, claim the promises in the Bible. Declare them out! Come on!'

I tried, believe me I tried.

After Meet Jesus Music concerts, I wielded Bible verses like the proverbial two-edged sword, no doubt inflicting grievous wounds and even chopping off a few heads whilst dispensing simplistic solutions to other people's problems. But I'll never know the results because I saw each of these people only once. My poor friends at least showed commitment to me. They kept trying to help, yet often succeeded in making matters worse—how frustrating! They prayed and prayed, they fasted, spent hours, months, a couple of years trying to help me. They consulted worriedly with each other and with 'experts'. They did everything they knew, yet nothing changed. My difficulties challenged—maybe even threatened—their levels of faith. Since they could hardly blame God, the fault must lie with me. None of us knew then that I was in no fit state to receive his help.

A kind vicar had become a friend and mentor. 'Do you *really* want to be set free, Lou?' He spoke gently, trying to help me, but had he not been driving at the time he uttered those chilling words, I think I would have murdered him. That night I wept on my knees, 'Lord, how *could* you have allowed him to say that to me?' But then he never realised how raw I felt, so raw that often I shied away in pain even from innocuous remarks. I don't blame that vicar, though my reaction to his words took me spiralling downwards for months. I don't blame the big name ministries who prayed for me. But I do ask myself now, where am I leaving people when I have finished praying for them or counselling them? In my experience, if someone is healed or set free from some demonic activity, it is pretty obvious. It will not help their faith to try to convince them that something has happened when it might not have done so. Most Christians suffering from chronic fear are already feeling guilty enough without some helpful counsellor hinting that they must be to blame.

Did I want to be better? My diary overflowed with my pleadings with God on the subject. I grabbed at any straw. Hearing some teaching about the benefits of being baptised in the name of Jesus, rather than in the names of the Father, Son and Holy Spirit, I wondered—could this prove a key to unlock my problems? Rebaptised according to the new formula, I felt no different.

They told me I needed more faith. Fear and faith could not both grip a person at the same time, but how could I find faith? I wished I could have stopped off at the supermarket to buy some! Friends had doubtless found their own advice helpful, when a little anxious about something. But deep neuroses held me in a grip too tight for reason's power to loosen. Fear affected the way my body functioned, everything. In fact I reckoned that I had become the very opposite of all a Christian should be. It never struck me that in fact I exercised enormous faith and trust in God every time I left the house.

I cannot remember anyone asking me, and I never asked myself, why I felt so frightened, so hopeless and depressed. Every time I seemed to conquer one fear, another would spring up to take its place. For example, if a slight pain twinged my stomach momentarily, I sweated for days in case it turned out to be the early signs of cancer. Once reassured on that, I imagined that the bus would crash, or that I would faint and fall off the stage during the next concert and break my back.

Then some new teaching surfaced. 'What You Speak Is What You Get.' If I shouted the verse about not having a spirit of fear loud enough and long enough it would become reality in my life. And it worked, so long as I stayed awake and kept the concentration going. For a period of several months I repeated this verse almost every minute of the day and, as long as I did that, the most dreadful fears stayed at the outer limit of my life. They still lurked, I could see them out of the corner of my eye, as it were, but by wielding the verse like a sword I could keep them at bay. It took all my energy, I couldn't do much else, but at last I had seen *some* kind of improvement.

Then one day I couldn't keep on battling any more. The fear was growing, pressing in harder than ever and I felt too exhausted to fight it. I realised that this was a crisis. God's enemy seemed to have succeeded in spoiling everything. I picked up my Bible and read a verse. 'In all these things we are more than conquerors through him who loved us.' Huh! Something snapped. I'd had enough of this nonsense. I hurled the big Bible across the room. It thudded against a pot plant and, as compost spilled out across the carpet, I thought wryly to myself that if I'd been living in Old Testament times I'd have been a heap of dust on the carpet by now. Even today good Christian girls never lost their temper with God! I waited. Nothing! Just my breathing and the hammering of my heart.

And then it dawned on me. Since becoming a Christian, even in my worst moments I reckoned that God had been holding some fear from me. Now that I'd thrown in the towel and given up on him, I could expect to be swallowed up, engulfed by unbearable fear, plunged into the abyss of insanity which I had dreaded ever since the bad trip.

But instead of a panic-filled abyss came a kind of grey nothingness, which lasted for two days. At the end of that time some words came into my mind, just as though they were printed on a TV screen. Very peculiar! I didn't know what to make of them though they seemed to come from God. He had spoken to me before, through words which other people prophesied, or through the Bible. In the past I'd spent many hours waiting, asking him to speak to me directly, disappointed when he never did. Now I had given up on God, the strange message was hardly likely to come from him. Or was it?

Still feeling grey and blank I wrote the words down and took them to a friend of mine called Faith. I knew that she spent much time in prayer and I was always fascinated to find out which world events the Lord was telling her to pray about. Six months later on the news I would sometimes hear the information which she had received in prayer well before the event happened. If anyone would be able to tell me if the message had come from God, Faith would.

Faith read the words I gave her.

I am so glad that you've given up now, Lou. Why have you been clinging so desperately to me while all the time my hands have been gently holding and supporting you? Rest. You have been saved by grace. It's time for you to move on and let me take over.

Faith glanced up at my anxious face and smiled. 'It sounds like God to me, Lou!' she said. At that moment I dared to begin to believe it. A flicker of excitement deep inside me heralded a resurrection of the hope which had slowly died over all those awful years of struggling.

In the days that followed I read those words over and over again and came to understand for myself a truth which I had known in my head since the age of four. Jesus *himself* would enable me to live his commands. I had no need to sweat and strain and worry in a frenzied attempt to become a good Christian!

Come to think of it, rest seemed an alien concept in our achievement-orientated society. I hardly remembered ever hearing a talk on the subject. Much evangelical tradition stressed that people should work for God. My parents sacrificed everything for him to the very end of their strength and beyond. Even the charismatic teaching which I had received encouraged me to lay hold of God's promises aggressively. God seemed to be telling me now that these things could only be done from a position of rest and of faith.

I started to read Christian writers like Andrew Murray, Watchman Nee and Charles Price. They insisted that we can never become what God wants us to be unless we receive and live in the Spirit of Christ, teaching our souls to wait on God. We should not demand from him in a frenetic fashion, but ask in active trust to be lifted up by his power. To someone as weak and powerless as myself that teaching felt like rope to a drowning man.

'Rest in me,' said Jesus, 'and I will begin to lift you up.' I had been taught to get into the word of God, to study the scriptures, and I knew the Bible backwards. But when Hugh Thompson ran a weekend on Bible meditation which I attended around that time, the one thing I carried away from it was, 'Let the word of God get into you.' Could this twist of a phrase explain why the Bible truths I knew so well had never really reached through to change me from the inside? From that weekend on I prayed the words of Ephesians 1:17–19, that I would have the spirit of wisdom and revelation to know Jesus better. Later I expressed this deep desire in a song:

> Open my eyes, that I may know
> All of those things that are needed to grow,
> Truths that your Spirit is longing to show.
> Open my eyes, that I might know.

Open our hearts that we may receive
Your gift of faith to help us believe,
Things that your word tells us of you.
Open our lives to live in your truth.

I wanted God's word to take root in my heart. I saw it now as a seed to be planted rather than as a truth to live up to. No longer did I think that if I behaved long enough in a certain way it would become natural. Only God could make his ways part of me, and without Jesus I could do nothing. Given sun and water a seed grows; it can't help itself! I knew that if I received the sun and water of God's presence I would not have to worry about growing— any more than a real seed does. I have always been grateful that God in his wisdom gave me this time before he began gently exposing and dealing with some of the knotty roots of my problems. He knows me and he knew how weak I had become at that period in my life. Right then resting in him was the only message I could have received.

God put in my mind a picture of a hosepipe which had become blocked with all sorts of rubbish. My efforts to unblock it had resulted in little more than sore fingers. But as I turned on the tap at the other end of the hose, the pressure of water forced the blockage effortlessly away into the drain. If I paid attention to the source of my life, to spending time with Jesus, the flow of his Spirit would begin to deal with everything which grieved me. Those who spend time with God can't help but become more like him. And so I took Humphrey (my big, green cushion), buried my face in it and began to wait on God. And, slowly, the orbit of my Christian life began to change. Though no overnight solution, these times laid a good foundation, giving me space in which to steady myself, to know God and to trust him again. My fears began to recede, little by little. God's perfect love, as it entered into my heart, began to cast out the fear that had made me its prisoner. God himself was beginning to set me free.

Later that month, something happened in a meeting which confirmed the changes which were taking place in my life. Morris Cerullo, an excitable Jew turned Christian evangelist, shouted at his audience from the stage. Emotions ran high in the crowded, noisy hall—just the sort of situation to make me nervous. Then Cerullo asked the stewards to shut all the doors and to let no one in or out. Instant megapanic came upon me—that scenario had to be the end for anyone suffering from claustrophobia. But suddenly I knew, quite simply, that God was big enough to cope—even with me! I have no idea of what anyone said during that meeting. I simply saw that though my life had shattered into fragments God did not expect me to collect them all up and glue them together. I needed only to hand each one to him, the craftsman who had made me in the first place, and breathe, 'Help!'

In the clamour of that meeting the Holy Spirit whispered to me, 'Why don't you give me your fear now? Only I can find the key. Leave it with me!' Suddenly my fear became God's problem. He had not been sitting in heaven, tapping his fingers impatiently, waiting for me to search my Bible day and night until I found the right verse to set me free. He had not turned his back on me in disgust while I failed yet again to find the right meeting or the right minister to work some formula which would banish fear. Suddenly a huge weight lifted as I realised that I no longer feared being frightened. Though the fear itself did not go at that point, much of the sting of it did. I no longer had to worry about finding solutions. I need not feel guilty, because my problems had become God's and he had the responsibility now for when and how to solve them. If I felt the fear creep up on me again, God would prompt me, 'Do you want to take back the responsibility for sorting this out, or are you going to leave it with me?' And even though it took time for the fear itself to go, I began to feel peace, real peace.

Philippians 4:6−7 came alive to me at that time. 'Do not be anxious about anything, but in every-thing, by prayer and petition, with thanksgiving, present your requests to God. And the peace of God, which transcends all understanding, will guard your hearts and your minds in Christ Jesus.' I see those verses as a real strategy, viewing 'do not be anxious' as a line which I must not cross. I must not take back those things which I have acknowledged to be God's responsibility. Often I battled in my mind over situ-ations for two or three days before I was prepared to let go, but the more I did the easier I found it. And today, when people pour out their troubles to me during counselling sessions or after concerts, I am very glad that I have learnt that those terrible weights are God's responsibility. I can then pray, in faith, that God will order the person's life to bring about the healing I know he wants—maybe through my words, using the limited time and skill I have, but also through the words, books, tapes of others, or in any way he chooses.

9
Touching Base

Many times I've kicked against the thing that held
    me down,
I'd come to you and weep and pray but it always
    hung around.
But as I see the way I am and face my deepest need,
I'm really glad you left me there to plead.

I asked for healing but you gave me the healer,
I asked for freedom but you bound me with love,
I asked for confidence but you gave me the Spirit's
    power,
And it's knowing that I need you keeps me by your
    side.

Looking back now, I almost regard it as a miracle
that God did keep me through the worst of those
months and years as a 'Crippled Christian', but I
remain grateful for all I learnt then. I know I have a
hard, impatient side to my personality. It took
experiences like those described in the last chapter to
create in me some of the compassion I would need in
order to help others effectively.

I moved on from Miss K's when another organisation took over her Refuge for use as a drug rehabilita-

tion centre, and went to stay with Pete and Beth Phillip, who lived with their four children and extended family near Tooting Bec. They were kind and I had a good time there. They put up with a good deal of insensitive, self-centred behaviour from me, because I never understood the pressures they faced, the demands on their lives both from people in the church of which Pete was curate, and from their young family. One of their children had Downs Syndrome. Previously, I had never known how to interact with people who had physical disabilities, but found that any fear or awkwardness soon vanished, and I have often felt grateful for the opportunity to get to know Christina.

The Holy Spirit was moving in the church, especially among young people. Visitors, including many students, often filled the curate's house. We held meetings there, and learnt to speak out the words God gave us to encourage others as we began to use gifts of the Holy Spirit such as prophecy, or the interpretation of tongues. Pete and Beth had big hearts. They created a free and friendly atmosphere in which we would launch into such things without dreading the consquences should we make some little mistake.

Some aspects I found slightly 'heavy'. For example, Pete decided that everyone in the house should rise at 6.30 each morning to pray together. Bright idea, appalling timing. I struggled enough to get through my day without this added pressure! However, the prevailing winds of doctrine were against me at that time. Someone had found the word 'authority' in the Bible and dubbed it flavour of the month. The Bible also equated rebellion to the sin of witchcraft. Game, set and match to church leaders! One girl shared my rebellious streak, so it came as quite a shock when she said one day, 'You never really give yourself, Lou!' Never give myself, I thought indignantly. I stay up half the night talking through people's problems! My friend saw how I was struggling with her comment and explained, 'I can't see you, Lou. You talk about the Lord, but never about yourself!' I failed to understand what she meant.

When the lease on Pete and Beth's house ran out, I moved in with a lovely Spirit-filled Catholic woman called Norma who lived near Clapham Junction with her husband and their four children. It must have been hard to squeeze me in as well. I suppose I provided some company for Norma and taught the children piano, but I never paid much towards my keep, or helped around the house. She even ironed my clothes, poor woman.

One day a man knocked on Norma's door and asked to see me. Once installed on the piano stool with a cracked coffee mug in his hand, he announced that he had come from ATV to ask if I would sing on a television programme. Shakily motioning him to a chair which faced away from my unmade bed, I sat at the piano and played a couple of my songs. I could hardly believe it when he said, 'Great, yes, just what we need for our Sunday programme!' He then solved the mystery of his sudden appearance by explaining that he had heard of me through Eric Delve, the evangelist who often worked with Meet Jesus Music.

Though I stayed awake all night in sheer panic, somehow God helped me glue myself together sufficiently to survive the ordeal of travelling to the studios in Birmingham and singing there. I had convinced myself that my efforts would go straight in the bin, but the bosses must have liked what they saw. They arranged for me to sing on three more of their Sunday night programmes, and later asked me to write and perform a song about Jairus' daughter for a programme called *Children of the Bible*.

In the midst of my constant battle with fear in London, I revised my opinion about Sidmouth. I had hated it for years, but now it became like a haven at holiday times. Its familiar streets posed no threats and the whole place felt so much safer than London. During my absence from Devon God had been busy! Some of the young people in my father's church had been filled with the Holy Spirit and they started spreading the good news about Jesus among hippies dossing on the beach. Many who came to know Jesus for themselves had been deeply involved in drugs and the occult. They threw up pastoral problems which no one in the church had come across before. My parents had been horrified when I prattled on in my usual insensitive way about how they needed to be filled with the Spirit and speak with tongues. Evangelicals from their background were taught that this experience had been ordained only for the time between the death of Jesus and the writing of the New Testament. Now we had the complete Bible we no longer needed supernatural gifts, they said, and viewed modern-day speaking in tongues as a dangerous, occult-inspired counterfeit. After some heated moments my parents and I reached a compromise by praying that the Lord would show one of us the error of his or her ways.

When my father saw the young people from his

church praying hippies off drugs, or waging warfare against the evil spirits which bound kids who had courted the occult; when he saw the remarkable and lasting changes for the better in some messed-up lives; his attitude towards renewal started to change. Seeing the young people move in a new, deeper dimension, he began to view the baptism of the Holy Spirit less as a threat, more as an exciting challenge. Both my parents began to enquire about it.

The West Country had became *the* place to go for the summer in the mid-seventies. Many hippies who came, all unsuspecting, to Sidmouth met with Jesus there. In the once-sedate little church whole groups went forward for baptism, long hair and all. Even the local papers showed an interest. Many hippies had nowhere to live. A couple from the church kindly lent their house, but we still had to feed large numbers. With growing excitement we watched the Lord supply food. All through that summer it happened the way I had read about in books. Great boxes of provisions appeared on the doorstep at just the right moment and we never did find out where they came from. Hotels phoned through to offer their left-overs at the very time our supplies ran out.

By the next year my father had invited a young man called Tony Rawles to work full time in his church as youth pastor. Tony, who had once been a heroin addict, helped open a coffee bar called The Haven. There many young people found new life in Jesus. They were set free from former lifestyles and habits which had become problems to them. Emmanuel Church and The Haven built up quite a reputation as places where God was on the move and, for a period of several years, drew people from miles around.

We held special missions during the Sidmouth Folk Festival. This week had seemed the highlight of my year as a child, because it brought so many people flooding into the sleepy little town. That year we held a week of prayer before the mission. We knew, somehow, that God was answering us—until the night when the mission was due to begin, when we felt a heavy darkness. It took persistence to battle our way through it in prayer. Then we heard faint sounds from the first folk procession. We began to realise that the festival with its fertility dances and other pagan rites could breed things which opposed the gospel of Jesus. I thought back to another such festival in Padstow and wondered if the unwholesome spiritual atmosphere there had had any effect on the beginnings of my relationship with Anna.

During school holidays I worked as youth leader alongside Tony. In Devon my life no longer revolved around a desperate battle with my phobias, so I found these times immensely fulfilling, which in turn meant my depression also lifted. At last I could begin to function on a spiritual level and I saw the Lord use me. Many of the young people whom I helped looked up to me, never realising how many problems I faced in my 'other life' back in London.

Then, through Norma, I came into contact with a little Roman Catholic community called Focalare. Rather than trying to learn the whole Bible without it affecting their lifestyle, Focalare took one scripture verse a month. The whole community meditated on that verse and asked God to reveal the meaning as they tried to live it out. At the end of the month everyone would share what they had learnt, not only in their heads but in their hearts, affecting their actions and emotions.

I had never seen such love shining out of a group of people before, or such profound simplicity in relationships with God and man. I could see it in their eyes and in their gentle approach. Focalare helped put me in touch with the contemplative side of Christianity, which I feel is missing in so many activity-orientated evangelical churches. God's word seemed to grow in that little community like a seed. For them Christianity did not consist in receiving a shot of blessing at a meeting. Its effects resembled less the sudden high of LSD and more the subtle effects of vitamin pills, slowly doing them lasting good. God's truth takes time to renew our hearts and minds.

Around this time Pete and Beth emigrated to New Zealand, which I found hard, because they had been like a spiritual mum and dad to me in London. Miss K, in her own inimitable style, had started rehabilitating the entire population of some town in Surrey. Aunty Peggy was occupied with her increasingly sick husband. I felt unsettled, bereft. Then, at a Meet Jesus Music concert I noticed a group of young people wearing flamboyant clothes and acting in what I can only describe as a more individualistic way than most Christians did at that time. They had found Jesus through a family called the Wilsons. I felt drawn to these larger-than-life people, who seemed to accept and love everyone. As I got to know them, it seemed a natural progression to move into their house, particularly since my fear had reached such a pitch that I had to stop work for a while. Showing unconditional love, they supported me right through this time, for which I am very grateful. Their oldest son, Simon, took me to MJM concerts, stood me on the stage and almost literally scraped me off it afterwards.

A man from the recording company, Word, had seen me sing on television. As a result we met to discuss doing a solo album, which meant decision time. I knew that I could not pursue both a solo career and one in the group. Yet even small decisions seemed impossible for someone as depressed and neurotic as I had become. I felt torn in two. In the end I decided to leave MJM, which found a singer to replace me and continued for a couple more years. Thrown back on God, yet again, I wrote a song.

> I feel the winds of change are blowing
> And nothing will be the same again.
> My spirit senses something new
> Though I don't understand it Lord.
> O Lord, if it were not for you,
> I couldn't see the future through.
> I need you here beside me Lord,
> I need your hand to guide me Lord.

My first solo album called *Don't Hide Away* ironically enough included some of my first triumphant songs. Doom and gloom had permeated much of my songwriting before then—hardly surprising given my circumstances. Yet I had found God faithful in seeing me through difficult times. He hadn't given me healing, though my experiences in Devon and with Focalare were laying the foundations for it. He had, however, given me the Healer, who walked through the darkness holding my hand, preventing me falling from the cliff's edge. I had no confidence in myself, yet the Holy Spirit did empower me, either to help others as in Sidmouth, or just to survive a very difficult time. I needed God and that need kept me close to him. Because I knew that he really did help me, some sense of hope stayed alive.

Deep down I knew that God was in control and I wrote these words.

> Weave on great weaver in the sky
> Although our earthly eyes can't see
> Complete the workings of your hand,
> Weave on that glorious tapestry.

I might only see a confused jumble of the various threads of my life. But God, from his side of the tapestry, could delight in the picture he had started weaving with the best silken threads and a sharp needle. I heard only the discordant sounds of a two-year-old let loose on a grand piano, yet God had a strategy for teaching the child to play beautiful music.

Did I choose *Don't Hide Away* as a title for my first album by chance? I don't think so. Even then I could sense that many people, many Christians, had whole areas of themselves hidden away—and occasionally someone sensed the same about me. On a human level, recording my first album involved incredible stress. To make matters worse, the music arranger had a heart attack the night before we started recording. (Strangely enough, some major crisis has happened in the middle of all but one of my other recordings, as well as during the work on this book.) But I don't think I would ever have finished *Don't Hide Away* if Simon Wilson hadn't carried me through.

I learnt a good deal from the Wilsons, much of which has stood the test of time. But all their love and very real support blinded me to the fact that isolated groups of Christians can, quite unconsciously, open themselves to dangers. In the end circumstances beyond my control removed me from their orbit. The relationship between Mr and Mrs Wilson broke down. Two houses were needed and there was no room for me. My dear friends, Geoff and Anne Hughes, took me in and gave me the love I had learnt to expect from them, but I gave in my notice and when my teaching duties finished that term returned home for good.

10

Reaching Out

Each man an island with a thousand passing scars,
Each heart a drawbridge on which others may not pass,
A thousand hurts driven deep within the soul,
Don't hide away;
Let the Lord know, then you can know yourself.

I found plenty to do in my father's church, taking on
pastoral responsibilities among the young people as
well as outreach through The Haven. Brian Rose-
veare, a local JP and landowner, had a large house in
Bovey Tracey where groups of young people
gathered to hear about God. Brian had been one of
the first people outside my father's church in Devon
to invite me to take an evening and he continued to
do so from time to time, once I moved down. I used
only a piano with no backing tapes in my early solo
performances, and never thought to include any
humour or up-tempo material. Those evenings must
have seemed intense affairs, all shade and no light.
Nevertheless, Brian seemed to sense something
worth encouraging. I value him as another of those

people who always believed in me even when I lost hope for myself.

I had met various people at Brian's house, which made establishing relationships in Devon easier for me. And I already knew Andy Hague through his wife Jo, a friend from Post Green days. Andy is still a great friend and influence on my life musically, because he has the ability to 'hear' eight or ten strands at the same time, to understand what I want from a song and to help me orchestrate it. His help has been invaluable in all my music, since my London-based *Don't Hide Away*.

I started leading Sunday worship in my father's church, playing the piano and introducing new songs. Because the Holy Spirit was moving, bringing warmth and life to the services, I found my role both enjoyable and fulfilling as I learnt to follow his leading. I felt that I belonged among this group of people and God seemed to be using me. Then one day I broke down in tears right in the middle of the worship—and I didn't even know why I was crying. The meeting ground to an embarrassed halt. Back home that afternoon I sat down at the piano and began to sing out what I felt.

> I feel lonely, deep down inside,
> You see my heart, Lord I cannot hide it.
> I need someone, someone to share,
> Someone to hold me, someone to care.

Me, lonely? No one could have been more integrated in the centre of church activities. But still the words came, putting me in touch with my inner pain.

> Lord I'm hurting, deep in my soul,

Under the smiling few people see it.
But your eyes, they pierce to the pain.
God of all comfort, heal me again.

How many more people felt this way, wearing a mask of Christian happiness, while crying silently inside? I remembered how one or two friends had intimated that they never saw the real me. Could this sense of inner isolation mean that I had surrounded certain parts of my true self with barbed wire so that people, and even God himself, could not come close? If so, I wanted to change and become real. I asked God to heal me, to help me reach out and become really connected again—to himself and to his people. The words of the song continued:

Give me the love that I need for my brother,
Healing the scars that we cause to each other.
Break down the barriers we build
To protect us from the wounds
So unspoken yet so real.
Lord you see just how we feel,
Oh Jesus, will you heal?

At last I wanted to make myself known, I wanted closeness, so the events which followed shocked me deeply. I noticed that my parents seemed concerned. Some members of the church had welcomed the Holy Spirit's renewal on board with open arms, to the point where they wanted nothing but to manifest the trappings of the charismatic movement. Another group took the opposite view, their long-held beliefs causing them to question the source of the new power. Those people caught in the middle, including my parents, never worried overmuch about what happened, so long as the Lord was in it.

Looking back, I still find it hard to grasp why the situation disintegrated in the way it did. Although renewal brings comfort and joy, perhaps the Holy Spirit also stirs up things in people which they have never faced before. I sensed that some church members' security lay in the structure of their religion, which left them inflexible when faced with change. And perhaps some power games were going on. In my travels around churches in more recent years I have seen things which reminded me of that situation and marvel at how complex people can be, how leaders often face a fierce battle to maintain harmony. Today, excellent books have been written on how to deal with conflict. But, back then, I only saw my parents becoming more distressed by the week. Those at the helm receive all the criticism. My father always considers what other people think and what effect his decisions will have on them. With three groups of people pulling three different ways, he became distressed that no matter which course he took he could not reconcile everyone. At times I wished he would act more like a dictator.

In the end the church went off in four different directions. Tony Rawles heard some teaching which said that God was moving mainly outside denominational churches in those days. He left our church and took most of the young people with him. Personally, I could not agree with him though he believed that he had good reasons. Our keen charismatic members aligned themselves to a fellowship in another town, while those highly suspicious of Holy Spirit renewal joined a little chapel up the hill. Only those holding the middle ground remained. The church took a long while to recover and continued to be cautious towards things of the Spirit, though they were to become a warm and loving congregation.

Feelings ran high during the whole process. Both sides attacked my parents, who were often unable to defend themselves because to do so would have breached confidentiality. Though not involved personally in the dispute, I hated to see them hurting so much. They must have neared quitting at times though further worries arose from the fact that our house was tied to Dad's job. Suddenly my parents, who had supported me though so much pain and trauma, were pouring out their hurts to me. My solution was to look for Christians of influence who would pray for them until I realised that no blanket prayer could make this situation better. I spent much time crying to God. 'I don't understand. They don't deserve this!'

'Watch, listen, learn,' God seemed to reply, very gently, 'and make sure you never treat anyone like some of these people are treating one another.'

So I continued to provide the music in church, however tense the atmosphere. Occasionally a lovely young girl called Debbie joined me, playing her cello. Debbie's parents were committed Christians who had worshipped with us for some time. I really liked the family. Myrtle, the mother, had fragile health but before long I sensed something else was wrong. It centred around Debbie's older brother. Steve was the black sheep of the family and worried them all because of his drunkenness, his womanising and the way in which he treated the family. Steve's dad, resourceful man, wondered if I might be able to help him, since I had been through similar things myself. When the family invited me to Sunday lunch at their home, Myrtle laid on a superb meal, but Steve, rather rudely I thought, showed up very late. OK, he had good looks with his fair hair and designer suntan, but I noticed how cold his eyes felt and how he failed to offer any word of apology or explanation to his parents.

Steve and I talked a little that afternoon, though I sensed he held back, suspicious because I was one of those Christians. Then I started to play the piano and I knew I'd found his weak point. He thawed enough to take me up to his room and play me some of his LPs. Over the next couple of months, Sunday lunches with his family became regular events for me.

By the time Christmas approached I felt exhausted. I had worked long hours in The Haven and longer still trying to help many of the younger people individually. Christmas Day fell on a Saturday that year and at church the next morning I heard something which made me angry. Steve's Mum who had been in hospital was let out early so that she could spend the festive season at home, yet Steve had arrived at their family Christmas dinner the worse for drink and had fallen asleep half-way through. Still drunk, he had crashed into the house late that same night and succeeded in waking everyone, including a baby nephew who was staying. Concerned that Myrtle, still weak in health, would be unable to cope, I offered to sleep the next night in Debbie's room. Maybe I could try to get some sense through to Steve? He came home very drunk in the early hours of Monday morning. Later, I took him a cup of tea and he complained of a monumental hang-over. Now that I had a captive audience, I laid into him.

'What do you think you are doing? You're not young, you're what, mid-twenties? How come you have no sense of responsibility? Do you realise the effect your behaviour is having on your family?' As I lectured on and on, Steve just sat there with his cup of tea, looking jaded, feeling too ill to offer any defence. 'What do you think I should do? he asked after a while in an attempt to escape from the situation.

'An apology to your parents would make a good start!' I snapped and stormed downstairs. A few minutes later, Steve, having made some attempt to tidy himself up, followed me into the living room. 'I'm sorry I caused a fuss,' he muttered to his parents, 'I'm off to work now.' He worked with a mechanic friend, buying and selling cars. Steve's parents just looked at me after he had left. 'That's the first time he's apologised in years!' Myrtle said. We began praying, yet again, for Steve. We all sensed a chink in his armour, but he had not stopped fighting. He told us later that he had in fact taken himself off to a party on Dartmoor where he started drinking straight scotches, one after another. But a strange thing happened. He felt more and more sober by the minute.

'Who the hell does that woman think she is?' he muttered to himself as he poured yet another drink. 'What gives her the right to say such things to me?' But no matter how he tried, he could not get drunk nor find any other way to switch off from the thoughts going round and round in his head.

The Lord gave me a song that day for Steve, but he failed to return home, and when he did, late the next night, he moved so quietly that I never woke. Next morning I found him, shoes in hand, trying to tip-toe out of the house without being noticed. I mentioned that I had written him a song and he came with me to the piano, his interest aroused in spite of himself.

You wake up in the morning and you find it's raining,
You start running away from the darkness inside.
But I've been hoping and I'll be waiting
Till you turn to the light and start running away into love.

You're so busy running that you can't see where you're going,
You're so busy fighting that you can't see the pain you're causing,
You're so busy lying that truth's become a stranger
And you can't see the danger all around you.

I turned to Steve. That oh so carefully cultivated look of detachment had vanished. He appeared vulnerable, as if someone had stripped his face off, and at last I could see a real person behind his eyes.

'Yes, well...' he said. Then we began to talk, and after a while it became obvious that he had been running, as so many people do, from a distorted perception of God. We prayed and Steve, in his own way, opened his heart to the Lord. It was time to bring in the spiritual heavyweights. My mind ran through those I knew searching for one who might have a reasonably broad attitude. The nearest lived in Exmouth. When Gordon prayed a few hours later, Steve was filled with the Holy Spirit.

Steve and I returned to his family home, but

before long he remembered that the girlfriend he slept with regularly was expecting him. As he left the house snow began to fall. His parents and I looked at one another. This woman would test the reality of what had happened to Steve. Five minutes later he returned. Instinctively I knew that he was coming back to me.

In the West Country, when it snows, it snows. Steve's village lay only five miles from my home in Sidmouth but already the road between them had become impassable. This worried me because my feelings were beginning to get out of hand and it was all my fault. I knew the rules—single girls should not get involved praying with men. I feared making life any more complicated for his family, or mine, so I kept wandering off into the snow, hoping that somehow it would freeze my emotions. I watched the sky and the weather forecast, desperate for the roads to clear enough for me to make an escape. 'Pluck these dreadful feelings from my heart, Lord,' I pleaded, with an enormous dose of melodrama, but the Lord plucked not.

Steve's parents had begun to sense what was happening and could not hide their delight. 'I've never seen him look at a girl like he does at you, Lou,' Myrtle smiled. Finally, on New Year's Eve, Steve and I admitted to each other how we felt and exchanged one lingering kiss. We both agreed about one thing. This relationship must be kept low key for a while.

On New Year's Day thick snow still disguised the contours of lane and tree and garden hedge, but the sun shone out of a freshly scrubbed blue sky. Steve and I wandered along by a little stream, the world's two most unlikely romantics. We paused by a frosted stile which sparkled as though it belonged on a film set.

'Marry me?'

'Yes!'

It was like being hit by a bomb. Our low key relationship had survived less than twenty-four hours!

Back home Steve's parents received the news of our lightning engagement with delight. To their credit my parents managed to hide the honest dismay which they must have felt at the time. I had walked out an unattached, single girl and returned a few days later with a nice-looking man who, in all fairness, had not exactly had the time to win his spiritual spurs. However, they soon came to accept Steve. The person who really had trouble coming to terms with our impending marriage was me. I struggled for much of the nine months of our engagement. Some of this was understandable. Steve had never, ever considered a woman's feelings before. It took him time to learn to hear and respect a female. Then, as a new Christian dragged right into the middle of an agonising church situation, he felt obliged to sit through church services because I had to play in them. Understandably, he resented this and often looked as black as thunder. Inevitably I felt caught up in the tension.

But my struggles ran deeper still. After Nigel, my artist boyfriend, had hurt me so deeply, I vowed that no man would ever come close again. Since the age of sixteen the only deep emotional attachment I had formed had been with Anna. And yet here I was engaged to Steve. Had it not been so sudden and had we not announced our engagement to the world while still on a tidal wave of emotion, I might never have married Steve—or anyone. Now, unwilling to go back on my public promise, yet unable to open myself to this man, I felt trapped. For years a pain barrier had bounced me back from any emotional closeness, but now I was plunging beyond that barrier, and for three days I felt submerged in something beyond my control. It started with a sinking feeling in the pit of my stomach, then revulsion, panic and intense mental pain took me over. I wanted nothing to do with Steve.

Friends prayed me through that time. My feelings did not dissipate with prayer, but I knew that Jesus walked through the tunnel of pain with me. At the end of three days I emerged the other side knowing that a battle had been won—that I could marry Steve with all the closeness of relationship which that implied.

Our differing personalities have always provided plenty of friction in our relationship, but in some ways we complement each other. For example, I am so grateful for his practicality, when I have virtually none. Loving my singing, he asked if I possessed a PA. I remembered a few bits under my bed, left over from MJM days. Digging around, we came across a few dusty wires, an amp and a couple of mikes. 'I've no idea how they work!' I told him. With a twinkle in his eye, Steve gave me a look which said, 'Helpless woman!' and disappeared with the assorted parts. After an afternoon's hammering and soldering he presented me with a working PA system—complete with some speakers he had bought. What a man, I thought, extremely impressed.

We used that PA for years. Its construction marked the beginning of the commitment which Steve has shown to my music ever since, though it has cost him in terms of both time and self-esteem. As we travel the country we have learnt that people who work behind the scenes, for example with lighting and PA, are the great unsung heroes of the Christian church. I believe that the Lord put Steve and me together as a team, to work together on every level, not just the practical one, and I could never have done all I have done without drawing on his many strengths. Back then, however, I only knew that he believed in my music, encouraging me to sing again, though I had done very little in public since moving to Sidmouth.

The Sheldon Christian Conference Centre in the Teign Valley had in its grounds the makings of an open-air theatre. Groups of volunteers had developed this over the years and, during the summer of our engagement, the Centre invited some local people who were interested in the arts to put on a play there. We formed ourselves into the Sheldon Theatre Company and continued to conceive, write and perform major productions there for the next three summers, plus some smaller ones at other times of the year. I sang many of the songs, and it did me good to turn outwards from pain-filled, self-centred material to serve a group again. Many songs which appear on my second album, *Walls*, I originally wrote for Sheldon plays.

As well as fulfilling his technical role with the equipment Steve acted in the theatre group too— notably as the angel Gabriel, complete with cockney accent! Our last production, *Messengers*, was net-

worked by national television on Christmas Day
1983. Our hearts warmed to the Sheldon group. We
learnt to be honest as we worked on the drama and
music. They showed sensitivity to one another's feelings as well as creativity. I respected them as people
who had their lives together and possessed a certain
street credibility. Their big hearts accepted Steve
and me. They became God's family to us more than
'normal' church itself could—especially at that time
when Steve fought shy of many of the trappings of
religion. I began to meet once a week with three of
the women initially to pray for the productions, but I
came to value above all the support which we
received from one another in prayer.

Our friends' patience must have been stretched to
breaking point by the melodramatic rows which
erupted when our personalities clashed. But they
were prepared to talk these things through with us in
such a way that we felt loved and helped, rather than
threatened or judged. We began to learn that we
could tell them how we really felt without fear that
they would respond with narrow-minded attitudes or
simplistic answers to complex questions. Maybe
their attitude gave us the courage to be able to face
some of our difficulties. In any event, some people in
that theatre company were to have dramatic effects
on our future.

II

I Know Where You're Coming From

Comforter, you are the Comforter
And I have pain inside my heart...will you comfort me?
The troubles of this world have torn my life apart
Man of sorrows, man of sorrows
Come and mend my broken heart.

After our wedding in 1979 we moved into a little house just behind the hospital in Exeter, feeling relieved to escape the tensions in Sidmouth! Steve started work as assistant manager in his father's business selling sheepskins; I gave piano lessons. In many ways we had a good secure start to our married lives, yet I found myself in turmoil.

As a single person I had enjoyed freedom to organise my life, to duck out of painful issues and to control circumstances which otherwise might have controlled me. Now, at the age of twenty-seven, marriage was demolishing some of my defences. Like many men, Steve handled conflict by taking himself off, alone, until he had calmed down and sorted out his emotions. Like many women, I wanted to work things through until we came to some agreement. If he disappeared, I started coming apart inside. The separation from Steve churned up something very deep within and triggered my old panic reactions again, making me run to find him. If Steve had not come to terms with his own feelings by then, he would reject me all over again and I would spiral even further downwards. I often needed to call in a friend to pray with me because I felt that I had no inner resources to survive.

New situations or major decisions triggered panic in me. Even setting a date for our marriage had caused problems. When we moved house the irrational terror became too big for me and I feared that I would never come through the experience. Then an American, who had heard me sing in Devon, invited Steve and me over to do a series of concerts. The thought of travelling to the States by plane and staying with strangers there spun me into another anxiety state. But we did go and I found that part of me enjoyed the experience, though deep down I longed throughout most of the trip to return home. By the final day I had reached the point of exhaustion. We arrived at the airport to discover that our plane home had been delayed for hours. For some reason Laker Airlines decided to feed us in a New York disco, where the pounding music and flashing lights brought back horrific memories of my bad trip. Still, somehow, I survived to tell the tale!

Back in Exeter I took driving lessons. It's not unusual to feel nervous at the thought of taking the wheel, but my lurking agoraphobia meant that it took a huge effort of will for me to stay in the car. I had little concentration left for minor issues like noticing traffic signals or selecting the correct gear.

Talk about the classic stereotype of a woman driver—the driving instructors must have fought each other not to teach me! I stuck at it, however, and must have shown some improvement for one day my instructor proclaimed it time for my mock test. I had already perfected the emergency spurt and came out with a classic. By the time some spectacular kangaroo jumps had culminated in my hill-stall I began to sense that things were not going well. After my twenty-one point turn, although I only mounted the pavement six times, the instructor stopped me— a bad sign. He took over the wheel and drove me home. It was time for a lecture and he did it very well.

Of course, I can laugh at it now, but at the time I felt such a failure. I called myself a Christian, yet my old fears still prevented me coping with something as simple as a mock driving test. The instructor had touched a raw nerve and only after soaking twenty-five boxes of tissues did I think of turning to the Lord. I wished I'd gone to him first because, after a silence, he spoke into my heart.

'Lou, I don't care what that man said. I know where you're coming from and I'm proud of you.' My loving Father's words set me crying all over again. The instructor had no way of knowing about my agoraphobia, but God had seen my struggle. How quick we are to apply standards, comparisons and judgements to other people—and to ourselves. Almost from birth most of us are programmed to believe that reward and approval depend on our achievements. But God loves us just as we are. His eyes are fixed less on what we achieve than on what we receive from him. After all, even the best of us are only accepted on the basis of the Cross. If we could see ourselves from his perspective we would understand that the worst of our problems never cause him to despair of us. Calming down at last, I poured the Lord's words into a song.

Maybe it looks like an hour's work
But it could have taken years and years.
Many a simple task in life
Has been crippled by doubts and fears.
People judge so easily, the surface things they see,
But the Spirit of God searches for truth and sees things differently.

I know where you're coming from, I know where you've been,
I know the whole world loves a winner, but I still love you when you fail to win.
Anyone can love a superstar who's learned to play the part,
But I'd rather have a poor man who opens up his heart.

I have met so many people who feel misunderstood. Maybe they have never been affirmed by their parents. Maybe work or church or friends have hurt them, but God understands. The Bible is full of people, like King David or Simon Peter, who messed things up well and truly, but God had an especial love for them and used them in amazing ways.

Around this time I saw the Sacred Dance Group act out the story of the first Good Friday. When the character playing Jesus walked in with his hands behind his back, the Lord spoke so clearly to my heart, 'I know what it's like to be bound.' Immediately I started to cry—he understood my struggle to be free. Satan sells us the lie, 'You're worthless, unacceptable!' What fools we are to listen! Of course,

I could come to Jesus and hand myself, complete with problems, over to him. On the Cross he took responsibility for everyone upon himself so that, if we only come to him, he can set us free. He copes with us not coping, and when we are sinning, that's when we should talk to the friend of sinners.

It still disturbed me that my fears kept surfacing again, however. My life had seemed more in control since leaving London. I had genuinely seen the Lord work through me, so why did he not help me now? I reasoned that my fear must represent something like the apostle Paul's thorn in the flesh—a sign that God still used me despite my weakness. Then, over a long period, largely through conversations with people in the theatre group, something began to dawn on me. I had asked the Holy Spirit into my life and he certainly lived within me. But, imagining my heart to be like a house, maybe I only allowed him into a room which I had specially decorated and tidied for visitors. Could I have other areas—rooms whose doors I locked, even against my conscious self, because I felt ashamed of the contents?

The second summer we worked on a Sheldon production, a sympathetic woman called Ruth Moss helped with the costumes and sometimes her husband, Roger, came along too. I avoided him once I found that he worked as a psychiatrist. He might zoom in with X-ray eyes on all the terrible things wrong with me! However, the love, honesty and acceptance of the group as a whole must have seeped through my defences enough for me to begin to share a little of the way I felt with Ruth one day. She invited me round to her home.

As we chatted there over a meal I found myself

opening up to Roger, saying things I'd vowed I would never tell anyone. I was amazed to see him listening with interest. He seemed to know what I was talking about, whereas most of my friends obviously felt out of their depth. After a while he paused, put down his napkin and looked at me, then said, almost to himself, 'I wonder why you're so frightened.' Such a simple question—and it had never occurred to me before! I knew then that I had to make an appointment to see him professionally.

Roger had done a great deal of research into the way people are affected by certain experiences in the womb and during early childhood. Happily, maternity hospitals today have changed. Feeding used to have to go by the clock, for example, but now those rigid, clinical attitudes have been abandoned because the 'experts' have realised the importance of establishing an early bond between mother and child.

Through talking and praying with Roger I gained a great deal of insight into some of my formative memories and experiences. We began to see that certain events, for example the early trauma which the doctor had treated with phenobarbitone, might have triggered a 'separation anxiety'. A child's panic at Mummy's disappearance had transferred into adulthood as an irrational fear of losing everything which made me secure. Thinking about my panic attacks when faced with travelling, or conflict with Steve, I realised that any separation from known security did indeed bring up deep fears from within me.

Roger never attempted to deal with the current level of panic in my life, but after two or three sessions spent with him certain areas changed distinctly for the better. Over the next six months many fears began to lose their grip. Even when one did surface I could now recognise it as part of the old separation anxiety whose root had been exposed and pulled out. It had nothing to feed on any more. Satan no longer had the power to turn those wounds rotten, to prevent God's healing resources being applied whenever an imagined rejection or small anxiety jolted me. I began to grasp the importance of leaving the enemy no room, no hidden, festering places, however painful the cleansing of wounds might prove.

At Roger's prompting I had entered a 'room' kept locked for decades. The child in me, who had remained trapped there, afraid to face the skeleton in the cupboard, could now be comforted by the Holy Spirit, the Comforter himself. The skeleton vanished in a puff of dust as the light of God's love and truth shone into that dusty room. My Lord helped me clear any debris so that I could come and go there at will, taking others with me, just as I would enter any ordinary room.

It had only been my respect for Roger as a person which caused me to listen to what he had to say, but later I found that my conversations with him had equipped me to understand people I met through my concerts. Unlike myself many people had known real, deep rejection from their parents. I could see a certain pattern emerging. The children who had been faced with certain sorts of crises came out with parallel kinds of behaviour as adults.

I met Maureen after a seminar I gave at a Christian holiday conference. She had come to know Jesus a few years previously, but life still seemed a struggle. Plagued by guilt that she did not 'triumph in Christ', and finding that church did not seem to give her the help she needed, she tried to push her negative feelings down. After she told me about her locked room of abandonment my heart went out to her and I wrote her a song—'Broken Heart'. I quoted some of it in Chapter 2. The first verses described how I imagined she must feel, the kind of things she might say to God if speaking honestly. I had never before written a song as though in someone else's shoes, but I wanted her to know that God understood. Jesus offered no easy answers in the shape of a happy Christian love-plaster to magically make her wounds better overnight, yet he brought hope if she would let him begin a healing process in her.

An unknown seed conceived in passion,
That lived and grew without a name,
That long before the cord was broken
Knew the world was steeped in pain.

Comforter, you are the Comforter
And I have pain inside my heart...will you comfort me?
The troubles of this world have torn my life apart
Man of sorrows,
Come and mend my broken heart.

I am still in touch with Maureen. The Bible says in 2 Corinthians 1:4 that whenever the Holy Spirit gives us special comfort in our particular pain, he enables us to comfort other hurting people. Today Maureen has found the Comforter to such an extent that the Lord now uses her to help others with problems.

I have found that whenever I have shared songs like 'Broken Heart' hurting Christians have emerged from the audience suffering from similar problems. Some are rejected at birth and put up for adoption. Others know they were unwanted because their parents talk about them as 'accidents', or maybe they grew up in unloving homes. But the truth is that every believer's name was written in the Lamb's Book of Life before the foundation of the world. Jesus wanted us and he is always with us through our human separations. Even though a mother may forget her child, the Lord will never forget us as Isaiah 49:15 says. If we had known God as children like we know him now, we would have heard his voice. But through the years other tapes have been drumming rejection into our heads and their effects will take a while to unlearn. A journey towards wholeness takes the form of a process lasting months or years, but I know many who have ploughed on and emerged the other side.

A couple of years into our marriage, Steve started talking about us having children. 'I'm not sure,' I hedged. Something in me reacted against the idea. I think I feared that they would invade my space and time, trapping my artistic spirit. However, the Bible talked about children as a blessing, so eventually I came to the conclusion that I had it wrong as usual. We went on to plan our family and I first found out that I was pregnant at the Christian conference centre of Lee Abbey. I was supposed to be lending Dr Roger Moss a hand, backing up some of his psychological insights by sharing from my personal experiences—but I seemed to spend most of my time in the toilet!

Those nine months of pregnancy proved stressful. Nearly every day, when Steve came in from work, I could tell something was wrong. When I asked he either exploded or muttered things about cash flow. The recession of the early 1980s had begun to bite, and to make matters worse, the VAT man was prowling.

'At least your father's honest!' I tried to comfort Steve, but apparently his dad used his head as the filing cabinet for many records.

'If the business goes under, that's two families' income gone!' continued Steve. I shared his anxiety, but tried to avoid mentioning new-found psychological insights about the effects which early experiences have on us. I knew enough to realise that my mother's health worries had percolated through to me in the womb. What effect would our worrying have on our unborn child?

Roger saw me one last time for a consultation and explained, 'It would be unrealistic to give your baby the message that the world is a cosy and perfect place. But you know that, despite everything, God is here and he loves us. Talk to your baby and tell him that.' Being a great talker anyway, I found it quite natural to chat away to the little person beginning to move and kick inside my belly—and to pray for him.

I had not expected the huge waves of joy I felt after Jacob's birth. I wrote 'Jacob's Song' for him— the first music I had composed for nine months.

> Life is a miracle, love is a miracle,
> And a miracle has happened to you.
> Life is a miracle, love is a miracle,
> And a miracle has happened to me.

I learned a great deal from having Jacob. I found I loved him unconditionally, and so understood a little more of how God loves me…and all of his children. At about eighteen months old, Jacob developed a very high fever, and lay in hospital with suspected meningitis. I ached for his helplessness and would have given anything to change places with him. Months after the crisis, God gently reminded me of that feeling. 'The mother-love you felt was just a tiny reflection of my love for people. You couldn't change places with your son. I could, and did, change places with my world!'

In more mundane moments, amid the everyday pressures of life, I have sometimes worried that I cannot always be there for my children. I will never reach SuperMum standards. Sometimes I lack time and space and energy to give my children the very best. In a fallen, imperfect world they are bound to suffer deprivations of some of the very things which God intended as their birthright. Roger helped me understand God's grace and protection. When we become aware of any particular issue, Steve and I pray about it as well as doing our best to put it right. And even if I can see areas where we as parents score 'C minus could do better', as a family I reckon we deserve 'A plus' for hugs and for expressing our love to one another!

So, to my surprise, I enjoyed family life, especially watching Jacob grow and develop, but I started asking some questions when I saw how he trusted us as his parents. I began to wonder how my own sense of trust had been damaged. On the one hand life had become so much easier now that I could handle most fears. But a vague suspicion began to dawn. Could there be more locked rooms?

12

Nightmare Room

You are a child, you are a victim,
But nobody taught you the world was at war,
You don't even know what side you belong to,
You don't even know who to tell.
So you lock it all up in your nightmare room
But you still remember it well...

Two days after Jacob's birth in 1983, Steve was made redundant. It had become obvious that the recession-hit sheepskin business could no longer support both his Dad's family and ours. We felt it only fair that Steve, being the younger, should leave, but it still came as a blow. What other employer would release him to help me whenever I had TV work, a concert or a theatre performance—and even lend the firm's van to transport our PA? Steve's Dad had undoubedly been good to us!

Three months after Jacob's birth I recorded my album *Walls* with a group of musicians called Flight. Making that LP involved a great deal of work for very little money (thank you all!). We did the final recording in Tiverton school with direct takes, which meant that five or so instruments had to be playing

exactly the right thing at the right time. To compli-
cate matters further, we had not appreciated when
we hired the hall that it would come complete with a
bevy of enthusiastic cleaners. The record's sleeve
should really have included credits to such people as
Amy—Mop and Bucket!

Going back to my early days of TV work I had
first appeared on television in the West Country in a
talent competition called *South West Showcase*, along
with Andy Hague and Laura Higgins, my brides-
maid. Having won our heat, we performed in the
final show-case programme. Chatting to the producer, Tim Watson, I happened to mention that I
was engaged to be married. He pricked up his ears,
because his friend John Bartlet had just embarked on
a quasi-religious project called 'The Seven Ages of
Man'. Eventually Steve and I featured in his programme about engagement—and made more contacts in the world of television. From then on I
worked regularly for the regional television stations
of the West Country. I have sung, spoken and interviewed other Christians. I suppose my face has
become fairly well known in the southwest because
occasionally I overhear strangers muttering, 'Isn't
that, er, what's her name?'

I became a regular presenter of *Nightcall*, which
had a miniscule slot every week-night at ten-thirty.
Large numbers watched, if only because no one
found it worth turning off their set for two minutes. I
found the preparation of the talks quite a challenge,
trying to make a telling point to such a wide audience
in so little time. I have appeared three times on
Highway both singing *and* being interviewed by Sir
Harry Secombe. And more recently the programme

Encounter networked a half-hour documentary about my life.

It was through another *Encounter* programme that I realised Marilyn Baker had made the transition from the blind student I knew at the Royal College to Christian singer. I found out that she was coming to give a concert in Exeter, and invited her to stay with us. We so enjoyed meeting again that we have remained good mates ever since. I was especially touched when Marilyn told me how my songs had changed her life, speaking into her need at the time. I was the first Christian songwriter she had come across, and she asked God if he would give her a gift of music to help others. Now I often hear of how she helps people who are hurting. These days Marilyn writes most of her own material but she still sings a few of my songs.

From time to time, someone comes up to me after a concert saying, 'You sang one of Marilyn's tonight,' to which I reply, very graciously, 'No, she sings some of mine!'

In Exeter we had a good giggle about student days. When Marilyn happened to bump into a record producer at College she enthused about my songs and lent him a tape. He liked it and wanted to see me. Just as we were going into his company's offices Marilyn happened to mention that he managed a pop group.

'It's got a biblical name,' she said. 'Exodus? No, I know—Genesis!' Shell shocked, I walked in and after being introduced to some of the mega-famous group who happened to be there, I had to play my songs. Amazingly, the producer liked them.

'But you'll have to change the lyrics!' he said. I glanced at Marilyn sitting next me on the sofa.

'I can't do that!' I said and, almost as a reflex action, began my standard gospel presentation. In truth, at the time the thought of launching into a world of unknown non-Christians scared me silly.

Which brings us back to recession hit days of unemployment in 1983. When Steve was first made redundant he loved staying at home. At last he had time to complete unfinished jobs around the house, time to spend with me and with our new baby Jacob. But it slowly dawned on him that, along with his job, he had lost much of his sense of identity and self-esteem. Society seems to say, 'You are only as good as your achievements' and I don't think most men realise the extent to which they pick up that message. I wrote Steve a song.

You've been walking in the valley of despair,
Wondering if I care that you're living in confusion,
But don't you know the breaking of your heart
Will open up the part that can shine with my reflection?

And love will never let you down, always be around
To catch you when you fall,
And light will never fail to come, bringing you the Son
And saying when you call,
'I am the way.'

I wish I could say that these words had a dramatic effect on Steve's life, bringing life and health to his dry places like rain on parched soil. He pronounced it a 'nice song' and stayed locked in depression! However, he did try to find help. Dr Roger Moss, being over-busy at the time, sent him to a very experienced friend. Gordon Wright had set up Cross Line, which offers Christians counselling at the end of a phone line across many towns and cities in this country. He also takes on more in-depth, one-on-one situations. Gordon was to become highly significant in both our lives.

In helping Steve come to terms with some problems, he realised that many issues concerned me, and asked if I could come to see him too. Gordon homed in with counselling far more systematic than anyone had ever offered me before. Roger had dealt very effectively with one area, but as I came to know and trust Gordon over the coming weeks and months, we began to cover other aspects in more depth. It took time, peeling each layer back like the skin of an onion, before I felt ready to move on to the next. Beneath some layers irritants lurked like pieces of grit. Although hidden, they had nonetheless grated away at me over the years.

I found that Gordon never recoiled in shock from any revelation, nor did I sense that he might betray my trust by passing on my confessions to other Christians even in the guise of 'prayer requests'. He never dreamt of giving easy, formularised answers to my complex questions, never jumped to put things right. Sometimes I poured out things which troubled me about myself, expecting him to pray for them. He refused. 'If I asked God to take those things away, it would be like asking him to change the way he made you!' he said. 'You say, for example, that your over-sensitivity hurts. It makes you vulnerable. But it also feeds your creativity and your ability to empathise with others. Do you really want God to take away those things which make you effective?'

I often believed that, if I could only find someone to say the right prayer, my life would change. It became my one desire at one stage, yet in meeting after meeting, people to the right and left of me would leap around, apparently healed, and I would stay the same. 'I've had a lot of prayer for things,' I said with a sigh. Gordon replied that maybe those prayers had helped a little—at best they had lopped the top off the weeds in my garden, as it were. But if we could find and destroy the root of the problem, its shoots and fruit would wither too.

As I grew to feel completely safe with Gordon I began to tell him things I had never told anyone before, secret fantasies which caused me shame. All the time I was scanning his face anxiously for a hint of shock or disapproval, and felt greatly relieved when I sensed only acceptance. He even assured me that other Christians had struggled with similar things. The way out lay, he said, not necessarily in a direct attack on the behaviour, but in dealing with the root causes.

The root! I think Gordon sensed before I did that many of my problems sprang from something deep and unacknowledged in my life, something in which I had participated, willingly or not. An event had happened in the past, so awful that my conscious mind had blocked it off even from myself. Gordon suspected that he knew the nature of it, but also realised that forcing the issue, or dealing with it prematurely, could prove harmful. He wondered if a woman might draw it out of me.

I was thirty-five years old when I went to see Sheila Smith, the Chairman of the Baptist Health and Healing Association. I had already begun counselling other people. I had earned quite a name for myself as a Christian singer and speaker. I had survived some major traumas by finding a way through them with God. I thought of myself as a reasonably mature and honest Christian.

When I met Sheila she prayed, inviting the Holy Spirit to come and show us the root of my problems. As we waited on the Lord, one sentence kept going through my head. 'I can't tell you, because I promised I wouldn't. I can't tell you, because I promised I wouldn't.' When I spoke those words out loud to Sheila it was as though I had found the lock of the door at last. Together we prayed that the sword of the Spirit would cut off any wrong vows or promises which I had made as a child. I 'heard' a threat. 'You'll be taken away from your Mummy for ever and ever, if you tell!' Those words, effective as they might have been against any young child, had tapped into my deepest nightmares of separation. I understood as an adult why the power of that promise had kept a dark secret locked up all those years.

As Sheila and I broke that childish vow in prayer, suddenly I knew that I had suffered sexual abuse as a child. The experience came back in vivid detail. But because I could not 'see' the perpetrator, I assumed him to be a stranger. We prayed—and I expected that, as with Roger's ministry concerning my early years, freedom would follow now that this traumatic event had been brought into the light of God's love.

Two weeks later, however, Steve said something quite small, which triggered hurt in me beyond any reason. The mental agony became so unendurable that I locked myself in the toilet and banged my head against the wall. My brain simply could not cope with the horror I felt. I returned to see Sheila and, as we prayed again, I had to face the fact that I must have known the person who had violated me in childhood. The abuse which I suffered had not come out of the blue from a stranger, horrible though that would have been in itself. God was revealing, little by little, that the abuse had taken place over a period of time and that the perpetrator, though not a blood relation, came within the circle of people whom my family trusted. That left far deeper damage stamped all over my body, soul and spirit. Its consequences had followed me down the years, colouring my view of myself, of other people and of God—of everything. The way towards wholeness from that kind of damage could only take the form of a long and painful journey.

At this point, some of you reading my story will start to wonder. Coming from a safe and loving Christian background, surely I must have been unfortunate! Well, my parents had warned me about 'strangers' of course. In fact Mum had so impressed upon me that I must never accept lifts from anyone that when some emergency cropped up and she asked a friend of hers to pick me up from school, I refused to go with him. Sadly, in those days no one appreciated how common abuse was, nor the fact that most abusers already have a close relationship with the child. Though statistics are notoriously difficult to compile in this area, recent surveys indicate that around one in ten adults in the UK suffered some unwanted violation of their sexual space during their childhood. Abusers come from all social classes and education levels. To all outward appearances they may be the pillars of society. Shockingly, surveys have shown that, if anything, abuse is more

prevalent within churches than outside them—
partly because parents trust other Christians, never
dreaming that they might do such terrible things,
even if their child hints at it. But some Christians do
secretly 'boil over' into this area, often those who try
in their own strength to live up to the high standards
which they set themselves.

In America, psychologists are beginning to con-
clude that many serious mental health problems and
personality disorders have the hidden trauma of
abuse as their root cause. Research in one prison
revealed that 65% of the inmates had suffered sexual
abuse as children. Yet even today, police and other
protective agencies in the UK think that only around
10% of abuse is ever reported, and even fewer victims
find effective help. Psychologists have found that
most children cope with the trauma of abuse by
denying it—a cruel twist since those who do talk will
end up much less damaged, provided that adults
listen and act appropriately.

I had been asking God what lay at the root of my
problem. He had been preparing me, first by building up my trust that he accepted me, no matter what.
Then I began to trust friends in the theatre group—
and on a deeper level, my prayer partners and my
counsellors—Roger, Gordon and now Sheila. Layer
after layer had been peeled back. As he gently removed
things which hurt me, God's healing love, and the love
of other Christians, poured in. Only now was God
allowing me to approach the central problem.

Interestingly I had written a song about child
abuse a few weeks before I realised its application to
myself. I had read a newspaper account of a chronic
case. Profoundly moved, I wrote the song 'Victim'.

Its first verse heads this chapter, but I want to quote
the rest of the song here, because it may be that some
who read this will feel an uncomfortable stirring that
something like this must have happened to them.
Like myself, they may be extremely surprised.

Few people talk openly about their personal
experience of abuse. It is too shameful. I find it
difficult. But whenever I talk about these things publicly, and especially when I sing this song, people
come up afterwards and acknowledge, sometimes for
the first time to any living soul, that they too have
been abused. Recovery from the effects of trauma is
never easy. Pain lives with you over a period of time.
But I have found hope and a way through. The first
step means taking down the defences which we erect
to protect our bleeding hearts.

Here then is the rest of the song:

You are a child, you are a victim,
But nobody taught you how to survive.
You don't even know why it has happened,
Don't even know words to describe
All the things that go on in your nightmare room
But you carry the pain in your eyes.

You are a victim of a world that is falling apart,
But sweet, bleeding victim, please don't board up your
    heart.

He was a man, he was a victim,
The battlefield of a world at war.
He opened his heart, gave up his life,
So that you could be freed from your nightmare room
And bury your pain in his love.

13
Dams and Deluges

Stone by stone you've built your home
And year by year the walls have grown,
You learn to make it on your own
And suddenly you're alone!

God had spent years and years in patient dismantling of my defences even to get me this far. All the
time he wanted to heal me, of course he did. I sat in
places where his Holy Spirit moved deeply, accom-
plishing mighty miracles, so why did I stay
unchanged? I believe that the little, damaged girl
inside me whispered, 'Don't trust!' God might have
given, but no way could I receive—certainly not from
some man who wanted to pray for me. A man had
broken my trust, and sometimes even the very male-
ness of Father God and Jesus had caused me to back
away.

Long ago the process of abuse had unleashed emotional forces which my child's brain was never
designed to handle. Like a computer overloading, it
triggered an automatic shut-down. Things which
had happened held such terror that I said to myself

and to others, 'What abuse?' until even I believed it never took place! Maybe that explains how I lived for thirty years in troubled ignorance. All too many trauma victims have similar experiences.

I adopted a strategy of building battlements to defend myself against the indefensible, and they worked against me. And after I became a Christian working in the media, how could I admit to problems? Especially when the standards which Christians demanded seemed so much higher than everyone else's. If I made even a small hole in the dam behind which my not-so-nice feelings seethed, surely the force of them would batter everything down—and who could stop the torrent of destruction then? My old nightmare returned—I would fall over the cliff's edge.

When God managed to ease away the last grip on my defences, all those lessons I'd learnt about God's unconditional love were tested to breaking point as everything within me screamed, 'You're unacceptable!' I did tumble over the edge—and fell about two feet into the strong arms of Jesus!

Admitting to myself and to another person that I had been abused were the hardest things I have ever done. I felt contaminated, right through. No one would accept me if they knew something this awful about me. God himself, in his holiness, would surely back away! I have since helped many people through this stage and most have reached desperate straits before they allowed themselves to open up. I am sure that is why God put me in a safe environment, why he only started the revealing and healing process when I had found a place of peace and safety with him—and had established a relationship of trust with people who could help me find his way forward.

We talk about strongholds of the enemy in our lives. I think that deceit, especially self-deceit, literally had a strong hold on mine. I am not surprised that I took the route of denial as a child—most do the same—but deceit is not God's way and as such it carries consequences, however good the 'excuse'. As I faced up to the large part which denial had played in my life I began to see how I had become adept at blocking off many things, beside the abuse and the traumas of early childhood. I blocked them off not only from God and from other people, but from myself.

As a teenager, I aimed to deceive my parents and others from the church. That led to rebelliousness and all sorts of hurtful consequences for me and for them. As a minister's daughter in Sidmouth, and even as a Christian evangelist in London, I built many mechanisms for blocking off large portions of my life so that I could pretend they did not exist. Like many young people, I took risks with sex and in doing so had to switch off to the sensitive side of my nature. My adventures with drugs and alcohol fed my fantasy that I had everything under control and had a successful strategy to avoid pain. When I started the affair with Anna I convinced myself that it could not be happening—until I ploughed in too deep.

Anyone who hides their true feelings behind a dam risks a burst, major or minor, when pent-up poisoned waters will spurt out, harming themselves and others. How often have I exploded in anger over someone's quite innocent remark, or spent hours in the toilet in floods of tears over some apparently trifling incident? In both cases I was tapping into feelings buried deep beyond my understanding, which surfaced sometimes in the shape of unease, anxiety, phobias, or pain. Sorting through some old papers, I came across that poem I wrote at Dartington, and could only wonder at the way my subconscious mind right back then had tried to give me clues to some of the terrible memories.

> …My mind is locked in some dark deed of yesterday
> A Domesday Book of all the deeds of hell
> Of happenings too terrible to tell…

Looking back at songs even from my early days as a Christian, many seemed to scream, 'Let me out, I want to be real!' Sometimes I wonder if our church environments reinforce denial when they allow people space only to express the Lord's victories in their lives.

Having said that, however, it may be dangerous to take down strong defences of denial before the person inside is ready to cope. I am always grateful that Gordon, my wise counsellor, did not come crashing in with his insight about my abuse. Jesus never forces our defences down, though unwise counsellors or other circumstances may. For example, I wonder if my bad trip on LSD took me beyond the walls I had built to suppress the terrible fear I had felt as a child, not only as a result of separation anxiety. Abuse victims often report feeling alone and defenceless in a big, hostile world. That intense isolation mirrors my experience during and after my bad trip, which had swept defences away without providing any kind of solution.

When finally I chose to release my dam, the patient, loving, accepting friends who listened to my outpourings for hours proved invaluable. I talked and talked and talked for months, round and round in circles, making very little sense, but I needed to get it all up and out. I needed someone to hear what no one had ever heard before. I needed to cry—tears which scalded me like acid with their bitterness at first, but later brought a strange healing of their own, as if draining me of some of the poison. A shut-down to pain and trauma had also meant a shut-down to enjoyment and love. Only after breaking the dam of silence, and letting all the bad feelings out, could room open up for love and laughter and self-acceptance.

By the time I found out about the abuse, I had become involved in a certain amount of counselling others—sometimes close friends, or people who responded in my concerts. Even as I was going through the painful stages of coming to terms with my abuse, God sent me several people to counsel. I had never come across a victim of sexual abuse before (or if I had, I never realised it) so when six turned up one after another I really didn't want to know. I had enough pain of my own, yet still they came, and I began to realise that perhaps God wanted me to help them. I felt like a teacher, driven to read the next page of the textbook every night in order to keep ahead of her pupils. But at least I understood where they came from. At least I could offer compassion because I had stood where they now stood.

Like me some abuse victims did not know that abuse lay at the root of the problem for which they were seeking help. A counsellor needs great sensitivity to understand when such people are stuck and when the time is right to help them find revelation. Methods differ and all counsellors need to listen to the Holy Spirit to find out how to approach each particular individual. The first, last and best strategy must make prayer central—that God will reveal it to the victim in his own way and time.

The very first step of facing the fact that I had been abused increased my pain rather than making it better, because it released all sorts of other feelings. Pain hurts! And I tire of Christians who try to sing and praise it all away, who try to make the sufferer deny pain by quoting scriptures, who look for a resurrection without a cross. The Apostle Paul wrote to the Corinthians that he had been 'unbearably crushed'. I reckon that, if he had written the same thing to some churches today, they would have drummed him out for lack of faith!

Jesus said, 'Blessed are those who mourn, for they will be comforted' (Matthew 5:4). He told us to weep with those who weep. Jesus walks with us through the valley of the shadow of death of Psalm 23, rather than zooming us round every obstacle on the mountain-top by-pass. In Psalm 84:6 the valley of Baca was a place of weeping—we pass through this valley on our pilgrimage to know more of God. If our hearts are set on him, the Psalm says, we will make Baca into a place of life-giving springs. Hosea 2:15 expresses the same thought about the valley of Achor (which means trouble.) The place had seen a shameful episode in the history of Israel, yet God promised to make it a door of hope.

But I say again; pain hurts, and I hate it.

I'm no hero, I like a quiet life,
Where everything is beautiful and everything is right.
I'm no hero, I never liked pain;
So meet me in the battle, Lord, and pick me up again.

For your school of love, it breaks me down inside;
Shatters my self-confidence and takes away my pride—
But then fills my emptiness with beautiful new wine,
Bringing healing to my body and renewing my mind.

I have found out things about God, about myself
and about other people, which I could have done no
other way than through pain. Isaiah 45:3 says, 'I will
give you the treasures of darkness, riches stored in
secret places, so that you may know that I am the
Lord, the God of Israel, who summons you by
name.' I have learnt most of what I know about God
in times of crisis. When I come to think of it, those
Christians whom I sense have some special, deep
relationship with the Lord, have forged it in times of
suffering. I think God allows some things, not to help
our own walk with him so much as to enable us to
reach out in compassion to others. We are called to
be priests, bringing God's goodness to those who
cannot yet find it for themselves. As High Priest,
Jesus suffered more than we shall ever do, though he
deserved it not at all. We are called to share a measure of his sufferings, so that later we will know the joy
of his resurrection.

Thank God that the dark valley comes to an end,
once God has transformed pain into something
which works for rather than against us. We do
emerge into a new day, to a place of light and colour
and plenty. His desert, made bearable by its sprink-
ling of rare flowers, becomes the lushness of a well-
watered garden.

A few years ago, one side of my stomach kept
swelling up and hurting. It troubled me especially
when I had travelled to take a weekend of meetings
in some church or other, so I downed paracetamol,

which numbed the pain enough for me to carry on. Each time I returned to Exeter and started resting, the trouble subsided. Then I had the sense to visit the doctor with full-blown symptoms and within a few days found myself referred to hospital. Initial panic died down when they found I 'only' had a blocked exit from one of my kidneys. The consultant explained that he would book me in for an operation to rebuild it. 'You won't like me for a few weeks afterwards,' he explained. 'It's a big operation, and painful!'

His honest words frightened me. I'd seen enough of nurses brandishing huge needles and chanting the old panacea, 'This won't hurt at all!' when in fact it hurt like mad. In truth, for a fortnight after the operation the agony far exceeded any I had felt before because the scalpel penetrated deep through healthy parts in order to repair the damaged area. Yet healing could not have taken place without it.

I came to see the difference between two types of pain. The first kind kept recurring but I managed to accommodate it as an ongoing part of my life. On the other hand the pain which I experienced after the operation was so acute that it brought dire distress and disruption at first, but eventually faded until it ceased to exist. Today I no longer have to give concerts and seminars through a blur of painkillers because the surgeon repaired the damaged part which had caused the problem. The kind of pain he caused me brought healing.

When Jesus read part of Isaiah 61 in the synagogue at the start of his ministry he shocked everyone be applying it to himself. Do read the whole chapter, if you have a moment. It's my favourite in the Bible, because it sums up all that God's amazing salvation means. He offers salvation from evil to wholeness, restoring us to a place of blessing once lost. But beyond that, God's salvation reaches a place where the pain once suffered takes on meaning, as damaged and devastated people become part of his redemptive plan for others!

> The Spirit of the Sovereign Lord is on me,
> because the Lord has anointed me
> to preach good news to the poor.
> He has sent me to bind up the broken-hearted,
> to proclaim freedom for the captives
> and release from darkness for the prisoners,
> to proclaim the year of the Lord's favour....
> Instead of their shame
> my people will receive a double portion
> and instead of disgrace
> they will rejoice in their inheritance;
> and so they will inherit a double portion in their land
> and everlasting joy will be theirs. (Isaiah 61:1-2,7)

One of my songs says, 'Only a fool would look inside if he had to stay the same.' Exploring the ruined, devastated places deep within carries such pain that, without God's promises of healing and restoration, maybe denial does rate as the best option. Secular counsellors encourage people to unburden themselves by talking about their hurts. But without God's love to heal wounds, without his help to deal with anger and shame, new-found openness can merely lead them to spew out bitterness, to become men-haters. That does not seem like healing to me.

I often visualize the cross as a large door which

opens to let us through to God. But it can also close, to shut us off from bad things in the past. I encourage people whom I counsel to see the door slamming to separate good from evil, freedom from captivity. Jesus empowers us to start anew on his side of that door, to escape from the cycle of destruction. Otherwise, the law of sin works so that the abused becomes the abuser—if not sexually, then in other ways. Jesus' redemption reverses the natural progression of evil, so that the abused can become a healer of damage!

We may feel weak and unworthy, following a downward spiral to sin and destruction, but Jesus can lift us up, making us strong and worthy. He saves us to the uttermost. For any of us, Jesus is enough! I wrote a song, based on Isaiah chapter 53, which explains what I believe he says to each one of us.

I was despised, I was rejected
So that you could be loved and always accepted.
I was forsaken, left all alone
So that you could be welcomed and brought back home.
See me, dying, bearing your pain.
You can be whole again.

Ever since I had decided to follow him, Jesus had been slowly convincing me that he had always carried a hope and a vision of what my life could become. His vision had never become frustrated by the damage which I had inflicted upon myself or which others had inflicted upon me.

Steve and I needed to move house a few years ago. We had certain requirements, but little money. When an estate agent friend showed us around a property, the first room we entered sported maroon walls, pink curtains and a purple carpet. As we toured other rooms we noticed ancient wiring and plumbing. Worst of all, the basement kitchen, dark and poky, adjoined a damp coal cellar and storeroom.

Back by the front door again, we glanced at each other, grinned at the estate agent, and said, 'We'll have it.' I could 'see' a music room; Steve could 'see' an office. The kitchen could be knocked through into the coal cellar to make an attractive and practical kitchen-diner for our family. Lurid colour schemes, plumbing, even structural problems could be changed. We had huge fun visualising the four-storey Victorian house. Potentially so full of character, it could look wonderful—given some work, imagination and tender loving care.

Steve, practical as ever, invested time and money in structural work on our new house. Visitors noticed only mess for months. Then a quick coat of paint after his hard work suddenly showed up some fine coving or the beautiful lines of a fireplace. Over the years, the house which we 'saw' has begun to emerge, until we feel proud of at least one or two rooms. My favourite music room, for instance, has plants and furniture which match both its style and our taste. In places, due to limited time and money, the original wallpaper still screams at us. But we will get there, one day.

When we first moved in, I learnt to adapt to the tiny kitchen. Somehow I squeezed essentials into the limited cupboards and made it work. When Steve announced, after a few weeks, that he was about to start knocking the walls down to create our new kitchen-diner, my heart sank. I had grown used to managing, but he raised his club hammer and the dust started to fly. For ages I had no kitchen at all. I could see no improvement and wished he had never started. But now we have a wonderful facility, with space for such luxuries as a washing up machine and a tumble dryer—a place where the children have plenty of room to play while I do the chores. I thank God for Steve who, despite my panic, pressed on with the plans and achieved the goal on which we had both agreed.

Our work on the house parallels the way God dealt with the deep root problems of my life. He took a hammer to some major structural defects, but only because he had confident plans for something far better. I protested and longed for the comfort of finding my nightmare room safely locked up again. But he, and some Christian friends who had cottoned on to his vision, saw me through until his good news could reach me, until the captive part of me could be freed. Eventually his light penetrated the darkness of my prison and his comfort soothed my grief. I will always carry certain scars—but then, so does Jesus! When I'm under pressure, they trouble me still, rather like the man whose broken leg, now mended, gives no trouble until he runs ten miles. But it's a comfort to know that even my scars can give hope to others who suffer, and point them on the way to redemption.

14

Healing Stream

Are you hurting, all broken up inside?
Frightened, thinking you just can't survive?
I love you, and I know what you're going through,
And I just want to carry your pain,
Carry it all away.

He was pierced for our transgressions,
he was crushed for our iniquities;
the punishment that brought us peace was upon him,
and by his wounds we are healed. (Isaiah 53:5)

The year 1986 found Lou Lewis, Christian singer and
evangelist, with three albums recorded and a number of TV credits to her name. God had already dealt
with many areas of my life and I had even begun to
pray for others to find wholeness deep inside. Yet in
that year, as a thirty-five-year-old wife and mother, I
finally acknowledged that I had been sexually
abused as a child. At times I still found it hard to
believe one huge area of my life had remained dead
and buried, so that for a quarter of a century, no one
knew it existed.

2 Corinthians 5:17 says, 'If anyone is in Christ, he

is a new creation; the old has gone, the new has come!' I found that verse hard to understand for, clearly, I had dragged much of the old into my new life. Now I began to see that, though Satan's main army had been dispelled from my life when I became a Christian, he found it easy to tempt or accuse me, because his guerrillas still sat posted in my areas of wounding. I had to make choices. If I received Jesus' life in those sore areas, I could no longer sit back and say, 'Well, that's just me—I'm like that because I've been damaged, you know!' I had to make sure all pockets of resistance within me, pockets where those enemy guerrillas could shelter, got rooted out. Or to use the house analogy again, I might have opened the front door of my life to God, but I still had to fling wide locked rooms to him wherever I found them.

When I became a Christian, Jesus spoke life back into me just as he did in Bible days with Lazarus. Yet I remained helpless and bound with 'grave-clothes'. Though Jesus called Lazarus forth and gave him life, it dawned on me that he asked his disciples, Lazarus' friends, to unwind the bandages which still wrapped the newly-resurrected corpse. Gradually off came the trappings and the smell of death. I could see that parts of me had already been freed through friends' and counsellors' prayer and care: others were still being unbound.

When someone suffers, two negative things can result—wounds and bondages. The wounds need to be cleaned and perhaps some ointment applied. Then they must be covered and the patient kept in an environment which will prevent reinfection while healing takes place. I have no idea whether Lazarus had any physical wounds, but I do know that I had plenty of emotional ones. They caused me to feel dirty, angry, confused and fearful. People had prayed about those wounds, had tried to 'cast them out'. But you do not cast out a wound, you heal it, or rather you bring the person to a place where Jesus can heal it.

But what about bondages—the grave-clothes that restrict us and keep us captive even after Jesus has given us new life? These are habit patterns. If I cut my knee, despite application of lashings of dettol and elastoplast, I use my leg in an awkward way which may spark trouble in the good leg or in my back. After a long-standing injury is healed, I may continue to walk with a limp from sheer habit. Just so, past injuries like rejection or abuse can cause us to function in a strange and often ungodly way.

For example, when an innocent child suffers abuse anyone with a shred of humanity will feel angry, because it is a terrible thing. But, as a victim, I off-loaded my anger on all the wrong people, simply because I found it too devastating to bear. That counts as sin, however good my 'excuse'. If this off-loading becomes a way of life—if I use it as my main strategy for channelling the red hot magma of my anger—sin may deepen into bondage. That needs dealing with, not healing. I needed to repent of the wrong off-loading of anger. I needed prayer for that bondage to be broken and help to find God's way to deal properly with the very real volcano inside. It's so easy to shift the blame, to exclaim, 'You are making me angry!' Adam blamed Eve; Eve blamed the serpent. I had to take back all the blame I dumped on others. Only when I said, 'I'm to blame for that row with Steve, or for my rebellion against God or my parents', could Jesus reach down his hand and reply, 'Yes, and I took the punishment you deserve.'

Looking back at the roots of some of the problems in my own life—the separation anxiety, the sexual abuse and the way in which I compounded the damage as I rebelled—I noticed some patterns emerging. Even though some of the people I counselled had very different hurtful experiences, I began to see similar effects which the damage had left in their lives. Even in my own case, if I try to work out exactly why things went wrong, no easy answers emerge. I can only assume that, both as a result of man's sin and of living in an imperfect, fallen world, hurts accumulate in many of our lives which leave us the prisoners of various damaging emotions and knee-jerk reactions. So I want to take time in the next four chapters to talk about the four main areas of wounding which I see most often—guilt, confusion, fear, and anger, and the bondages or behaviour patterns which often result from each of these.

So let's begin with guilt. When I let Jesus into the nightmare room of my past abuse, I chose life, but that involved awaking to the pain of very terrible wounds. I knew that God intended the sexual act to express the closeness and commitment of mutual love. Paul took it as an analogy of the union between Christ and the church. How then could anyone have used me in such a perverted way for his own sexual pleasure? That must have been all that I was good for, I reasoned. I must be so worthless, abnormal, or plain unlovable that I brought the abuse on myself. Alternatively, could I have been too pretty and precocious? In any event, it must have been my fault, or

I would not feel this foul and contaminated. So I argued to myself, round and round in circles.

Most abuse victims I have met seem overcome by a sense of guilt and contamination. If self-worth is measured on a scale of one to ten, they register minus eleven. I myself felt particular shame because I had enjoyed some of the things associated with the abuse. I co-operated, not only because the man threatened to take me away from my mummy, but because he gave me attention and sweets and he took me out. My counsellor helped me to see the seduction process which a man had used on a young child who had no knowledge, no wiles of her own. The pathetic reward of sweets had not motivated me towards abuse. I had never willingly participated in evil in order to enjoy it; nor had I invited it because of my childish dimple and winning smile. With the knowledge I have now as an adult, I could have stopped it happening—but as a little one I was unable to. I could no longer hold myself to blame!

I began to see that any guilt I felt over the fact that I had been abused had to be false. Facing up to the issue with an adult's perception helped. If it had come out in the open earlier, if the person had admitted responsibility for his actions, I would not have felt the same way. A child can easily assume guilt for the wrong things—for his parents' divorce, for example. That guilt may affect him for years until one day he has the courage to talk about it and finds that he had believed a lie all along. Then he will realise that family tensions sprang from his parent's warring, not from his childish naughtiness. I began to see that whenever I failed even in little things as a parent to my own children, I needed to apologise and admit my own fault so that they did not take it upon themselves.

Though my counsellor chopped truth's axe clean through one root of all my problems and showed it to be a huge lie, still I found it hard after all those years not to see myself as contaminated. In most cases, when we feel dirty and ashamed it is because we have done something wrong. We can confess it and take it to the Cross where Jesus will forgive us and wash us white as snow. Sin and guilt are not a problem to Jesus—he has given us the solution, freely, once and for all, if only we will accept it. But the guilt which I had felt about being abused had been false guilt, so I could not confess my sin at the Cross. I began to see that I had been covered with someone else's filth— that was why I felt dirty. If someone splurged vomit all over me, what would I do? Wash it off. I came to see how Jesus understands our intense feelings of shame and contamination, because as one totally innocent of any sin he took the filth and evil of all humanity upon himself voluntarily in order that we might be free of it. Through him, victim and sinner alike can be restored to a place of purity and wholeness again.

My young children enjoy their bath. They laugh and splash, roll and soak, I too enjoy luxuriating in the warm, relaxing water, forgetting about everything else, letting any tensions slide away. If someone I counsel feels unutterably dirty I ask her to picture herself walking across a field full of cow pats. Someone pushes her head first into the stinking mess. Then, in the distance she sees the house where Jesus lives. When she knocks at the door, he looks at her, not crossly, but with concern. He asks her in and goes to run a bath. She hesitates to bring the mess into his beautiful house, so smiling he lays some newspaper for her to walk on. Then he hands her a bin liner in which to put her soiled clothes and leaves soft, clean ones warming for her on the towel rail.

I see Jesus as a healing stream, which never runs dry.

> I am the Healing Stream, come and bathe in me.
> I can wash you clean and set you free
> For in my body there is the spirit and the blood.
> Believe in me, believe in me, believe in me,
> I am your God.
> Let it go... Let it go... Let it go to me.

Some of my wounds were healed through a long series of counselling sessions—and I still find help through counselling. Roger revealed truths about separation anxiety then Gordon took me further. Sheila finally helped me see that I had been abused and others, including Lin Button who helps both Steve and I today, have worked on other areas. Much of the healing of the wounds of feeling dirty and unlovable, however, came through ordinary Christian friends and prayer partners who offered unconditional love and acceptance—the most healing things in the world. They covered me with comfort, they listened without ever being shocked, they acted in the unenviable role of safety valve for my emotional outbursts, they nursed and protected me through my convalescence, giving me time and space enough to kick and grow. God could best reach through the tangle of my emotions when his people demonstrated his love and grace in a tangible way.

God longs for us to 'love our neighbour as ourselves'. Ultimately, damage matters because self-haters cannot love well. I had certainly found it hard to love, to give myself—who would want me? I could share Jesus, yes, and verses from the Bible, but now I began to understand all those people who said, 'You never give yourself, Lou!' I needed to confess this wrong attitude to the Lord and ask for his help. Learning to love myself and others has been a process, and funnily enough, all the hurt has softened my heart and has helped me understand more of what others go through.

As I have said before, sometimes God gives us a special level of faith for an individual—a real vision of how they can become, and of their potential in Jesus. I thank God that there have been several people, counsellors and friends, who have held that vision for me at times when I have lost sight of hope myself. They communicated the fact that, though they knew about my difficulties, they viewed me with joy and excitement, not as a walking problem area. More recently, I have seen people whose lives looked a complete mess and the Lord has given me a vision for them. In fact I hesitate to take on a new counsellee if I do not have a growing sense of what they may become in God.

Over the years, the Lord has given Steve and me a special love for certain individuals whom we invited into our home. In the early days we helped them most of the time, but today our relationship is no longer one-sided. They have become our dear friends, and we hope they see us in the same way! I wrote this song for one such person, Billy, just after I met him for the first time, when God impressed upon me the way he saw him. Both Billy and the song retain a very special place in our hearts.

I believe in you and the things you can do,
I see the finished picture because I'm the master painter,
And my hope never ends, I am your true and faithful
    friend,
On this you can depend, I believe in you.

But out there in the world
Where the vision's always been blurred
Men have put you down, left you fallen on the ground.
But I speak into the pain, look in my eyes, rise up again,
Open your eyes, open your heart,
For I believe in you.

Just as dirty wounds attract flies when they are left to fester, Satan, the lord of the flies, is on the prowl, looking out for gaping spiritual or emotional wounds to infect still further. He will use them to create bondages which inflict yet more damage. We all carry wounds, self-inflicted by our own sin or by the sin of others—and some of the things which I am going to mention are only extreme examples of things which we all suffer. For instance, we all have experienced rejection from time to time, but sometimes wounded people can adopt habit patterns which make them more and more easy to reject.

In the previous chapter I wrote about some bondages which come as a result of the wound of feeling dirty—things like deceit and suppression. Feelings of dirtiness which came in through sexual abuse penetrated to the very centre of my soul, robbing me of any sense of purity and innocence. Some people as a result become frigid sexually, but like many others, I adopted a promiscuous lifestyle, while keeping emotional involvement at bay. Why not live up to my own image of myself, using my looks and figure to grab power and my sexuality as a tool to manipulate and control? Sex itself I found disappointing, but it helped me get what I wanted out of people.

Much of my sexual behaviour changed after I became a Christian—at least after my affair with Anna ended—but even today I still find battle-grounds, especially in the area of sexual fantasies. Christians seldom write or talk about this problem, yet surprisingly many struggle with it. Over the years I have made ground, but have to say that, when I find myself under pressure, it can be one of the first things to give. So I have found no simple answers, except to say that I am learning, as I did with my fear, to give myself to the Lord, dirt and all, asking him to help me in his way and time.

Behaviour from the past caused its own problems. I had slept with people who were into drugs and the occult—and that carries consequences. We are more than physical beings. The two become one in more than just a physical way. I now believe that one gains a certain spiritual inheritance through any illicit sexual union, because the soul bonds in some way to that of the sexual partner. Certainly I have needed prayer to cut off unhealthy influences, for a spiritual dimension and a spiritual being lie behind the evil of abuse. In Ephesians 6:12 Paul writes, 'Our struggle is not against flesh and blood, but against the rulers, against the authorities, against the powers of this dark world and against the spiritual forces of evil in the heavenly realms.' God has given us spiritual armour for the battle, including the sword of the Spirit, which is the word of God. We need to wield that sword sometimes to cut off certain influences in our lives as God reveals them to us. Otherwise the original wound, hidden and festering, causes patterns of behaviour which themselves lead to more wounding and infection. And so we spiral downwards.

I have seen, both in my life and in those of other people, how such wounding can attract disaster of one kind or another. Often this takes the form of revictimisation, where the abused child perhaps grows up and marries a violent and abusive husband, or becomes a rape victim as an adult. Many seem to set themselves up for more abuse and rejection—as a counsellor, you can see it coming. Some even go on to become abusers themselves. I am amazed at how often those things happen. Satan is no gentleman—he kicks those who are down, he twists the knife in the wound.

Psalm 23 talks of goodness and mercy following me all the days of my life, but some people, even Christians, experience the opposite of such blessing; they live under a curse. Abuse victims, in particular, may attract far more than their share of totally unconnected disasters—maybe chronic illness or a series of accidents in their family. This may result less from the wound itself than from wrong lifestyles which they have adopted as strategies for coping. Those who indulge in such things as the occult or illicit sex inadvertently put themselves under the curse of sin. But on the cross Jesus took all our curses upon himself in order to set us free. Repentance and faith-filled prayer reopen the path from curse to blessing.

Having mentioned that spiritual influences can reinforce our problems, I would like to emphasise that the last thing a wounded person needs is Christians swarming all over her casting out spirits which she never had. I have left too many 'deliverance' sessions feeling frightened, angry and humiliated.

Though I had asked for prayer, my original problem remained and now I deduced that I must be 'possessed' as well! At that point I either slid further into depression or became blithely irresponsible about my sin—the devil made me do it!

The word 'possession' tends to frighten us, perhaps because horror films portray it as turning people into zombies controlled by forces of evil and unable to exercise any free will of their own. The word used in the Bible would be more accurately translated 'demonisation'. People may be influenced to a greater or lesser degree by the forces of the enemy. Our bondages—our continual habit patterns of sin—can allow enemy forces room and influence in our lives because they feel at home there. They may, to a greater or lesser extent, inhabit or 'demonise' people, yet those people still exercise some free will.

Jesus is able to liberate us from the influence of the enemy as well as from our sinful habit patterns which caused the problem in the first place. Sometimes these things scare us, but we have no need to fear because, 'The one who is in you is greater than the one who is in the world' (1 John 4:4). We may not get better overnight—but it will come.

I have found true deliverances always very undramatic. The acid test of them comes in real change, not in the spectacular nature of the event. When someone I trusted has prayed about some hold of evil on my life, on a few occasions I have felt something begin to come up within myself and have co-operated in prayer. I know something has gone because of the huge difference in my life from then on. In a sense, deliverance is the easy part—bringing someone to the point where it will remain effective takes time and effort. God's timing helps as something buried many layers deep may prove impossible to move at first. We need to discover what our real enemy is so that once the evil is banished we can ensure that we yield no room in that area again.

15

Anger

Father, I forgive him, let it go,
You know he hurt me, wounded me so.
The devil tempts me, 'Curse him and die!'
But Father of mercy, to you I will cry.

'In your anger do not sin.' (Ephesians 4:26)

When I found out about my abuse, after overwhelming feelings of dirtiness surfaced, anger took me over—total, blinding fury. I felt a rage towards all men because, for the first time as an adult I saw the horror of what one man had done to a child—to me. I saw the consequences of his actions working their pain-filled way through my life. It just wasn't fair! He had even caused the intense pain I felt now, as my broken dam spewed churning muddy waters for miles around. Previously I had accommodated hidden anger through a sinful way of life, which held me in its bondage. I hated a self which I saw as dirty, different, unlovable and violated. Now that I could no longer hold its torrent back, I began to realise how much the anger pent up behind the dam had been turned against myself.

I off-loaded more and more of it onto other people—my family, my counsellors, anyone who crossed my path. Hatred of men broke over me in waves, serving as a defence mechanism to guard my sexuality, my very being. If a workman in the street dared to wolf-whistle, I covered him in contempt and scorn because, in my agony, I simply found it easier to hate than to hurt. I have seen the same thing happen with so many others, especially incest victims who, because they cannot hate the person who hurt them, will off-load their anger in the strangest of places.

My mind seethed with furious questions which had no easy answers, though as part of the process of facing up to the damage of abuse they did need to be asked. Where had God been when the abuse took place? Why had he not stopped it, or at least given my parents some clue that it was happening? Only when we approach God with honesty can he lead us to a place where we begin to trust him for our rescue from the problem and are able to praise him again, even if we never fully understand why certain things had to happen. The Psalms are full of people pouring out agonised, angry questions to God. He can take it. He understands anger. His own heart cries out at injustice and at the abuse of the innocent. 'No,' he says, 'it isn't fair and it isn't my desire. But then, is it fair that my Son should have died so that you could be forgiven?'

I don't believe that God abandoned me during the abuse, or when the seeds of separation anxiety or other troubles were sown. He has certainly not abandoned me since, even though I have tried to run from him as fast as I could go. But evil permeates the world and he has given human beings free will to ally themselves to that evil, if they so choose.

If I look at the Bible as the broad canvas of God's dealings with mankind throughout history, I see his plans to redeem evil's damage and to restore man's relationships with himself and each other. Those plans have been frustrated so many times. Yet God never gives up, he simply makes a larger plan, so that more people are saved and redeemed. Fortunately we know the end of the story. He wins. Evil dies. Every tear is dried and nothing will mar our everlasting joy in an environment every bit as good as he always intended it should be. The lion will lie down with the lamb, and a little child—wholly loved and wholly safe—will lead them.

The central pivot of God's strategy in all of this seems to me to be forgiveness. Without that he would have given up on all of us long ago. So, how about me, if I claimed to be a follower of Jesus—could I forgive my abuser? What a question, when the sin seemed so immense and unforgivable, when the anger still raged within me! It took me a while, with lots of help from patient friends, to see that my present fury never hurt the man who abused me. After all, I didn't see him any more. But the anger did hurt myself. It hurt my dearest friends and family, and it hurt God, who had helped me through so much. Eventually I came to the place where I found it possible to ask him to make me willing to forgive.

Let me tell you about 'Kate'—a composite of some of the people I have counselled, in that everything in her story happened to someone I know. Kate's grandfather, a respected doctor, lived with the family, abusing Kate for seven years of her childhood and adolescence. At the age of thirteen she became pregnant by him. When she could no longer hide her body's swelling from her parents, she had an abortion and complications resulted. Now she may never be able to bear children.

Christians told Kate that God would not forgive her sins unless she forgave her grandfather, a statement so insensitive they might as well have nailed her in a coffin. I told her, 'I think the reverse is true. Unless you understand the forgiveness of God, you can never forgive your grandfather.' What else can one say to such people? Gently I asked Kate, 'Will you let go of your hatred, of your desire to hurt your grandfather—and allow God to judge him in his own way? Because, as it is, your anger hurts everyone else but him.'

She did let go. That was all she needed to do. Forgiveness does not mean making excuses for evil— the actions of Kate's grandfather were inexcusable. Nor had he ever asked for her forgiveness. At first we do not always feel forgiving—those feelings follow later, bit by bit. God requires only a letting go of our 'right' to hurt, to take revenge. That step feels more difficult than a leap to the moon, because it means taking down the defence systems which we have built to cope with our anger. But God requires that letting go before he can give us a real, supernatural ability to love.

One day I was counselling another friend whose father had abused her. After we prayed I asked if she could forgive her father. I could hear the child in her voice as she spat out, '*No!*' I asked her if she could visualise the Lord right there in the midst of all her terrifying memories. She described the compassion which filled his face. And then I prophesied what I felt Jesus was saying to her. 'What you see there in my face mirrors the way I created fathers to feel towards their children. If you are going to hate, hate the destroyer behind all this evil—the one who corrupts men like your father.' After that, my friend found the power to forgive.

Once, more recently, we were travelling to a concert when Steve said something which touched on a sensitive area and really hurt me. I knew I could not stand up in the concert and help people in the power of God's Holy Spirit unless I forgave Steve. So I laid down my anger—and promptly picked it up again! Resenting him gave me something to do with my strong emotions. Hating seemed so much easier than hurting. I had to choose to lay down my resentment as each wave of it came upon me—and the struggle would have ended in defeat, I think, if God had not dealt with the great root of anger in my life.

Those people closest to us can hurt us the most, because we have certain expectations of them. Even while writing this chapter tensions arose, sending me to bed angry *again*. But before I fell asleep, I realised that, in the last resort, I did want to be true to what I had just written. 'Help, Lord!' I prayed. 'It's been a hard day, and I feel too weak to pick up the sword of forgiveness tonight!' I woke up next morning, still cross. 'It's not fair. If I forgive this fault in so-and-so, will it all be swept under the carpet again, Lord?' But I had asked God for help and I found him faithful, because he softened my heart and sent his Spirit to help me—and together we won another little battle for his kingdom.

God tells us to hate evil—to hate the evil actions a person does, but not to hate the person. It works at all levels. Sometimes my son Jacob comes running to me after some squabble, 'I hate my sister!' he yells. 'No, Jacob,' I point out, 'you hate what she does to you sometimes, but really, you know you love her.'

I have met people who have faced up to their abuse through rape crisis centres and other secular means. They have come to an honest appraisal of the damage done to themselves, but they ooze anger and bitterness, which goes on to poison their lives and relationships. Even anger against God, while it needs honest expression at first, can become sinful self-indulgence, because God has provided a better way.

I know how hard it is. I felt so vulnerable even thinking about dismantling my long-standing defence mechanism of hating men. When I do choose to let it go, however, I find a new ability to relate to them properly, as a woman, in the right way. I also found a new ability to forgive myself, to begin to love the person I am, even though I don't always like what I do.

The song from which I quoted at the start of this chapter concludes with Jesus speaking.

> Father, forgive them, let it go,
> The pain is killing me as my blood flows.
> Be gone, deceiver, I break your chains.
> Receive your healing, in Jesus' name!

The power of forgiveness excites me. It's not a passive thing! Men inflicted physical, mental and spiritual agony of the Son of God, though he had done no wrong. They betrayed him and mocked his calling. They strung him up for all the world to see his dying agonies. And yet he forgave. Satan thought he had won at the very moment which proved decisive in his defeat. Incredible divine forgiveness released salvation for all of us. God transformed the apparent defeat of his plan into the event which would guarantee his final victory.

All through church history, forgiveness seems to have been one of the keys to releasing the power of God. The book of Acts describes how the first martyr, Stephen, forgave the men who stoned him. Soon afterwards God's power dynamited into the life of someone who had been there, encouraging the stone-throwers. That man became the Apostle Paul, who spread the gospel throughout much of his known world. Nearer our own time, look at Corrie ten Boom, who endured a Nazi concentration camp where her sister died. Their crime? Sheltering Jews. Years after Corrie left Ravensbruck, a man came up to her to shake her hand after a church service. He explained, brightly, that he had been one of her guards and that subsequently he had become a Christian and wasn't it wonderful? When she remembered how he had tortured them all, she struggled to respond, yet God helped her to face and forgive him. Corrie ten Boom had a profound effect on many countries of the world. She spoke many words and wrote many books—yet she said that her account of the incident which I have just described had the most impact in changing lives.

I have come to the conclusion that, the more huge a crime committed against an innocent victim, the greater the power released if they can later forgive. I often see things in picture form. I see wronged people wielding the sword of vengeance. But it is a double edged sword—dangerous to the user and to innocent bystanders. Then I see the wronged person handing his sword of vengeance over to the holy wrath of God. In turn he receives the sword of forgiveness, to accomplish good. Thus a vicious cycle is broken, the strongholds of God's enemies are pulled down, not built up, and the kingdom of heaven gains ground once robbed from it by evil.

I also began to see what to do with anger because, despite exercising forgiveness day by day and hour by hour, anger still surfaces, especially when I learn of others who are abused. It surprises me that I've heard very few sermons on the subject, because God can be angry and jealous and all sorts of things we think are not very nice and 'Christian'. The Bible tells us, 'In your anger, do not sin.' I began to see that evil should make us angry. It makes God angry. A not so meek and mild Jesus whipped the money changers out of the Temple. Jews are often passionate—what has happened to Christians? We should direct our righteous anger against evil, and boost our energy for the task of co-operating with God in defeating Satan's strategies. For example, it can be a long and sometimes draining process to help other people through the effects of their trauma. Why not get angry as we pray to bring down the enemy's strategies which have messed them up? At the very least our anger against the father of evil will add to our determination not to have our own lives wrecked by him. In Jesus' name I can curse the roots of bitterness, anger and resentment in my own life.

Why not, when they have damaged many innocent people, beside myself?

As to the mega issue of whether reconciliation is possible with the abuser—in my case I've no idea where he is. But I think that 'happy sticking-plaster' Christians need to exercise wisdom here. With a criminal offence such as abuse there are procedures to follow. So if, for example, a church discovers incest within one of its families, they may talk to the perpetrator. He could profess repentance and the child might forgive. But churches have come unstuck where they have healed the wounds lightly and failed to inform the authorities, where they have assumed that the situation has resolved itself. Once the dynamics of abuse have started they are difficult to stop. The victim's tiny plant of healing is fragile at first—and what abuser can be sure of the outcome should he return to a situation of temptation? Reconciliation would be wonderful—and surely God's ultimate desire—but we must be careful!

I have also known adults who pressed for reconciliation with their abuser and received fresh wounds, all the more terrible. Victims need strength before their forgiveness is tested in this way, before they make themselves so vulnerable again.

One day, talking in a small church group, I happened to mention the subject of abuse—in passing really. A little later, I noticed a girl of about eleven, sobbing. I comforted her and prayed for her in tongues, because she would not tell me her problem.

As we were packing up to go, I noticed a man hovering, as though he had something difficult to say. After thanking me for my talk he explained that he wanted to tell me something which he had never told anyone before. He had been a Christian for several years, but previously he had been an abuser. I froze inside and started taking about three thousand steps back. 'I don't want this Lord. I don't feel ready to face an abuser!' Yet there he stood, so I grabbed hold of Jesus' hand, as it were, and began to talk to him.

Before long I felt the Holy Spirit say something to me, very strongly. So I asked the man, 'Have you ever forgiven yourself?'

'No,' he replied, head down.

I looked him in the eye. Something stirred deep inside me and I said, 'Then, as an abused child, I forgive you, in Jesus' name!' We both started to cry from a very deep place, and then we hugged each other. Often abusers have some trauma in their own past, so I prayed about that and prayed that any bondages might be broken. I went on to advise him to see a counsellor I knew who lived in his area. Then Steve and I left the church.

A few weeks later my counsellor friend rang me to say that it transpired that this man had not only abused children in the past, but was still abusing his step-daughter. Who was she? The eleven-year-old girl who had sobbed in the meeting. I felt terrible. Talk about hearing the Holy Spirit! How could I have been so blind? Surely I should have confronted him, yet I *forgave* him! I gave myself hell for weeks until a letter arrived from the man—now in prison. 'Thank you,' he wrote. 'When you forgave me in Jesus' name that day, something broke in me. For the first time I came to terms with what I was doing. I admitted to myself that I've abused children all my life. I never thought of them as people, you see, but as things to be used. I've never been able to love until that moment when I felt love—God's love and your love.

'I called myself a Christian because church activities served as good cover. My second wife loved me, yet for years I hurt and betrayed her and her children. The day I met you I shed the first tears since my own childhood, and I didn't cry for myself, but for my victims. At that point, I knew that God had forgiven me, but I couldn't live with the weight of guilt. I had damaged young lives and broken the law of the land, so I gave myself up to the police. I knew that I faced hatred—justified hatred—and a prison term, but I also knew that no one could take God's love away from me. He has given me the courage to bear the consequences.'

That man is doing a long term inside, but we still correspond. He has found a living relationship with Father God and I have been able to put him in touch with other abusers who want to change, because he can help them where I cannot.

He made me think. If statistics show that so many children are abused, then all of us must know several. We must also know abusers. There may be one, or more, in each of my concerts and seminars. I need to realise that God hates the sin in them and the damage it does to their victims, but also that he loves the person and longs to set them free. Maybe they themselves were abuse victims in their own childhood, as is often the case. What will break the cycle, where the sins of the fathers are visited on the children unto the third or fourth generation? God chooses forgiveness and the Cross, strange stumbling blocks though they seem at first sight. All of us are sinners. The depth of the sin as we see it makes no difference to God. He stretches out his hand to save us all, making a pathway of hope for abusers too.

16

Confusion

You've been walking in the valley of despair,
Wondering if I care that you're living in confusion.
But don't you know, the breaking of your heart
Will open up the part that can shine with my reflection?

'You will know the truth and the truth will set you free.'
(John 8:32)

If talking about shame can seem in itself shameful, I have found writing about confusion a highly confusing task. So all I can try to do is to show how confusion built up in my own life, the effects it had on me, and then how God's truth set me free.

As a child I knew that Mum and Dad loved me very much, yet my father's work prevented him from spending as much time with me as he would have liked. My mother's health sometimes caused our separation and also prevented her from giving me some of the cuddles which I needed as a small child.

Our parents told my brother Paul and me that Jesus wanted to bring freedom into our lives, to make them richer and fuller. Yet they themselves worked to the point of exhaustion, made huge sacrifices, and the churches they served sometimes treated them badly. Of course, now I understand the paradox involved, that without death new life will not spring forth, but that paradox fails to make sense unless the person of Jesus breathes life into it, and I did not know Jesus in that way as I was growing up. Instead of the truth of God which might have set me free, I absorbed only warped perceptions. They didn't make sense and I felt disillusioned.

As I grew old enough to think for myself, I found myself confused by church teaching that it was wrong to behave in certain ways. Whole families of people at my school enjoyed time spent in pubs and cinemas while appearing to remain quite normal and healthy. I couldn't see them tumbling into the pit of hell simply because they did those things.

Then Dartington left more mixed messages. Beautiful and idyllic, it presented fantastic opportunities to study music, yet some of the most unhappy people I have ever known lived there. Also at Dartington, I found it confusing that adults had implied that mortal danger awaited any who came near drugs, whereas cannabis seemed to have less effect on me than socially acceptable alcohol.

Any trauma in childhood may leave strong messages of confusion, especially that of sexual abuse. My abuser told me that what he did to my body was OK. I had strong feelings otherwise, but I lacked a reference point, because I never discussed the matter with anyone. Subconsciously, it had left me feeling so different from other people that I never felt I belonged in any group. Like so many children who become isolated or alienated, for whatever reason, I used fantasy to pretend that everything would be all right…when I had my Very Own Pony, when Romance swept me off my feet, when the world fêted me as a Concert Pianist, or when I became Best Friend of the most popular girl in the class.

A later escape route meant sexual fantasies, both romantic and dark ones. With Nigel, the artist, I thought I had discovered the romance of my dreams. He said he loved me. He treated me with great sensitivity—looking back I see him doing the opposite of what I had experienced in abuse. But that avenue of hope, like so many others, led to profound disillusionment when he rejected me, and caused me to cut myself off even more from my true feelings. My depression deepened every time I related to people who didn't really care about me. When I set myself up for more hurt at their hands I only confirmed my cynical view of the world and erected stronger barriers which prevented any who did care from reaching me.

I hated being alone and sought approval with such desperation that I became whatever I thought people wanted me to be—artistic, sexy, amusing, outrageous. I could act the parts well, though somehow it never quite worked—at school I stood out as the Vicar's daughter; at church, as a rebel. At age sixteen, if anyone had asked the real Linda Hayles to stand up, about ten of me would have exchanged worried glances round the room. Then a little voice right at the back might have whispered, 'Well, actually, I don't know who I am!' The outward show of my image, from clothes and mannerisms to attitudes, became the only 'me' that even I really knew.

Ambivalence and confusion result in more depression. In the end who was I? A nothing, alone in a vast and hostile universe. That thought opened up reality beyond bearing. Drink and drugs helped blur the pain. I've known others turn to different sorts of compulsive behaviour—eating disorders, sexual peculiarities. Some people split off from reality altogether, becoming schizophrenic.

Because I cut off from certain painful areas in my life, as I grew up I continued to use fantasy in ways which eventually proved dangerous. Drugs at first helped me to escape moral choices and to pretend that all was fine. Later, when I sought transcendental experience through LSD it nearly killed me.

Because of my confusion about right and wrong I often tried to re-run something I knew to be forbidden in the hope that it would bring pleasant feelings with it this time. Part of the lure of my lesbian affair lay in the secrecy surrounding actions which I saw as forbidden and shameful. Some of its attraction would have been lost had I not hidden it even from my free-thinking friends at Dartington. And within the secretive intensity of that relationship I really felt like I belonged, for a while. I lost my sense of overwhelming loneliness, because someone shared the forbidden thing with me. For once in that period of my life, I allowed myself emotional closeness with someone, which was why Anna's loss devastated me so much. I had to forgo the good as well as the bad in that relationship, and no one filled the gap for a very long time. It might have helped if people in the church had understood what it cost me to end my relationship with Anna.

Maybe because I enjoyed certain aspects of being seduced by my abuser, somewhere deep in my child's heart, the wires of pain and pleasure became crossed.

Good became bad, bad beautiful. My cynical eyes viewed the unsophisticated love and simple happiness of Christians as contemptible. Dabbling in the occult, or waking stoned out of my head on LSD in some dubious area of Notting Hill, I saw as free and wonderful and 'right'.

Isaiah 5:20-23 says,

> Woe to those who call evil good and good evil,
> who put darkness for light and light for darkness,
> who put bitter for sweet and sweet for bitter.
> Woe to those who are wise in their own eyes
> and clever in their own sight.
> Woe to those who are heroes at drinking wine
> and champions at mixing drinks,
> who acquit the guilty for a bribe,
> but deny justice to the innocent.

I cast myself as a superior young rebel, forging a new path. Yet almost 3,000 years ago Isaiah wrote about people who had behaved in a similar fashion—and it carried consequences. Old wounds might have been at the root of the reason for my rebellion, but the fruit tasted of plain old-fashioned sin—and the wages of sin is death. In my case, but for the grace of God, I believe death would have come quite literally.

Fortunately, I had a strong, loving family, and in the end they proved a major key to helping me. But children of broken marriages, for example, can often end up confused, as can those who constantly move around the country or world. Even the twentieth-century phenomenon of the nuclear family, split off from grandparents, aunts and cousins, can add to the feeling of rootlessness which some children experience. And, of course, in our increasingly secular society, few stand on the bedrock of faith and so have no secure place from which they can begin to understand the world.

God intended the parental bond to provide the roots of our security and the basis of our view of the world. That bond is perverted in the worst way by incest—and extremes of confusion result. How can a person learn to relate to other human beings in love when their primary source of love had been tainted with evil? What can someone do with his or her feelings towards an abusive mother, father or brother? Love and hatred seethe in a red hot cauldron, yet will not mix. Some have told me how they wished their abuser could have been a stranger for then they would have had a clear enemy. Such abuse often comes, not with violence, but as a warped expression of love. These incest victims have no clear enemy to hate and many go to great lengths to protect their abuser. One wrote in a poem,

> Loving too much to hate, hating too much to love,
> My mind beat itself to death
> On the bars of betrayal.
> A house divided against itself cannot stand.

The wounds are heart-chilling, the subsequent damage often grotesque, and yet I have seen people whose lives have been ruined in this way come into a place of wholeness again. So how are all these wounds healed and how are the bondages broken? If truth sets us free from confusion and lies, what is truth? Even a powerful ruler like Pontius Pilate failed to find the answer, because truth is not a 'what', a thing, or a system which our minds can use to make sense of the world. In my father's church we used to sing,

> I tried the broken cisterns Lord,
> But, ah! the waters failed!
> E'en as I stooped to drink they fled,
> And mocked me as I wailed.

Paul and I laughed about this hymn. We had only come across cisterns in toilets and anyone daft enough to drink from those deserved trouble, we thought. But, of course, the words refer to Jeremiah 2:13, 'They have forsaken me, the spring of living water, and have dug their own cisterns, broken cisterns that cannot hold water.' Having rejected Jesus, I spent years looking for the perfect cistern to satisfy my growing thirst, becoming more and more confused as each dried up or became bitter to the taste. An old proverb says, 'You can lead a horse to water, but you can't make him drink.' Some wise person quipped, 'But you can gallop him to make him thirsty.' After all my hectic strategies failed, when I reached a point of total desperation, I found my lost identity in Jesus. He, not a thing but a person, is the way, the truth and the life. I have found that many confusing paradoxes, and all the little disparate fragments of insight I have gained along the way, start to make sense only in relationship with him.

Long before I came to terms with separation anxiety, or with the fact that I had been abused, I found a growing sense of security in my identity as a precious child of God. This became a bedrock which helped me through the various dambusting experiences. I had become a Christian out of an acute realisation that I could go it alone no more. I had been brought face to face with the reality of helpless aloneness in a hostile universe—with hell, if you like. So the discovery of a loving father in heaven came as good news indeed. He filled the universe with his warmth, he upheld it by his power, and yet he cared about me.

Later, when I tried to do things right as a Christian, I nearly gave up. I struggled against all the damage which my wrong ways of coping with my wounds had caused. When I did let go, God began to plant his word of truth like a seed in me. Words from Ephesians chapter one verse 17, were some of the first which began to take root as I meditated on the fact that God was giving me 'the Spirit of wisdom and revelation' to know him better. He would 'enlighten the eyes of [my] heart,' in order that I might 'know the hope to which he has called [me], the riches of his glorious inheritance in the saints and his incomparably great power for us who believe.'

It was as though I had spent years playing tapes inside my head which brainwashed me with repeated lies—that I was dirty, perverted, unlovable. I had no value and would never belong. I had to keep quiet. I had to develop strategies to survive on my own since the system of morality, the Christian worldview which I had received from my parents, had failed me. Now I needed to play 'tapes' which repeated truth—to allow God's word to grow in me, to read it and meditate on it, to allow room for the amazing truth of it to come home to me. As I began really to *know* the truth of those words from Ephesians in the heart of me, not just in my mind, the truth of them began the process of setting me free. I remember the day, the very spot when I walked around Sidmouth, praying quietly, and I suddenly realised that Christ really was *in* me, my hope of glory!

So who am I? The daughter of a loving heavenly father. How can I relate to others? With the same, honest, self-giving love which he gave me. Is bad beautiful? No, because God has set out his moral code very clearly. Like a manufacturer's instructions it was written for my own good and (amazing, this) *he helps me keep it*.

Developing a relationship of trust with people took time. I am so grateful to those who patiently helped me through. Along the way the hob-nailed boot brigade caused certain setbacks, but the unconditional love and self-giving of so many individuals in the body of Christ acted as a lifeline. I no longer needed a mask to hide my empty face, an image to hide me from reality—though various defence mechanisms had become such a way of life that I still have to consciously step away from them sometimes. For example, I can don my mask of professional performer, who has it all together, though I hate people to put me on a pedestal as a being somehow different from them, just because I stand up at the front and spout. So normally I smash my mask at the start of concerts and seminars by suggesting that, in some areas, individuals in the audience may be way ahead of me. But I also say that if they had known me five years previously, they would have been surprised at what God has done in me. If any of them knew me ten or fifteen years ago, they must realise that a miracle has taken place! I only hope that, if they meet me five years in the future, they will see more evidence of the grace of God at work. And I sing,

I am just like you, a blind man searching for the sun,
Praying that you will come upon my journey

As to confusion about sexual identity, I had to make a choice there also to follow God's way. I found that hard, and I think the church needs to be aware of how much grief and struggle can be involved. But again, the prayer of friends like Miss K helped cut me off from spiritual ties to Anna and, after I first became engaged to Steve, prayer helped me through the pain barrier of allowing myself to relate to him so that I could start to give my whole self.

Because of my wounds of confusion I had indulged in certain forms of behaviour, and the results of these needed sorting out. Any involvement with the occult needs repentance, because it allows willing entry into the kingdom of the evil one. Prayer, the blood of Jesus and the sword of the Spirit cut me off from any continuing influence. The mind-expanding drugs in which I had indulged seemed to affect me more than did direct occult involvement. In fact, of all the mistakes I made in my life, taking LSD is the one I most regret. My occult dabbling did not go very deep, but LSD opened me up to all kinds of horrors. People tell me that it actually destroys brain cells. I know that certain sci-fi or psychedelic films still disturb me, deeply. In some ways LSD has marked me for life, made me vulnerable to spiritual invasion in the same way heavy exposure to hypnotism or the occult might. Although, again, prayer has restored much and, if nothing else, my experience with LSD taught me to depend on God.

An excess of alcohol and soft drugs arrested my emotional development. In that crucial stage of teenager-becoming-adult I retreated into a happy haze to avoid facing decisions. After becoming a Christian, I think many of my struggles had to do with growing up emotionally, with learning to make moral choices and to accept responsibility for their consequences, rather than retreating into the fantasy world which I had embraced in my confusion. My Christian 'adolescent phase' proved as up-and-down and long-drawn-out as that of a real teenager. But then, so many of us have areas of our inner selves which still resemble a wounded child and consequently have much growing up to do.

If we look to find our identity in the people or things around us, at best they will shore up for a time the growing fissures in our self-esteem. Leanne Payne, a writer whom I much admire, calls this being 'bent towards the creature'. Damage from the past can strike at the very roots of our being with horrific effects. But, in reality, only God can tell us who we are, because only God truly understands our hearts. In his presence the rotten bits of us begin to fall away, and the true self he always wanted us to be thrives in relationship with him.

17

Fear

And as a flower to the sun,
My child, I would have you come,
And as a baby knows no fear,
Draw near, and you will feel no harm...
One day you'll see...
From broken, tuneless harmony
Will come a brand new perfect song.

'Cast all your anxiety on him, because he cares for you.'
(1 Peter 5:7)

I have told the story of how fear built up in my life.
The early experiences which I described might not
have affected all children, but in my case a vivid
imagination served to magnify any little worry.
Later, abuse led to more fear, which I pushed down,
way out of sight, until one drug trip released all the
terrors with such force that they continued to para-
lyse my life, even as a Christian. The Bible says that
perfect love casts out fear. As a new Christian I
assumed those words meant that, if only I could
summon up enough love for God, my fear would go.
It is just as well that Jesus' big hand has always held

me tight, because my puny grip on him faltered so many times. But the stranglehold of fear loosened as Jesus poured his love in and in and in to me, until I learnt to receive it as a free gift.

Music reminded me of his love. I might read a book or listen to a tape of a Christian talk once, or maybe twice, but music tapes I played again and again and the affirming truths of their inspired words built me up. Because other people's songs have helped me, I love to learn of occasions when my music has helped others—just as I prayed it would all those years ago in London. One day a stranger came up to me after a concert saying, 'You saved my life!' Apparently, she had been incredibly low and on the point of committing suicide when something drew her attention to a tape which she had never played before, one of mine which a friend had lent her some time previously. She played and played and played it all night. By the morning she knew that she did not want to die and even felt strong enough to go and find help. The tape had intervened at a cross roads in her life and pointed her on the way to recovery.

On another occasion my father asked me if I could help a doctor who had phoned him saying she needed to talk to a minister. She had incurable cancer and feared dying. I talked with her and afterwards God used a tape of my songs to assure her of his love and to help her to find a relationship with him. Eventually she reached a deep conviction that she would wake from the death of her body to new life with Jesus. At the end she sank into a semi-coma, but the tape still played. Every time it stopped, she stirred and whispered, 'Music!' until her spirit finally passed into heaven.

As to my own fear, I have written about various ways which I believe Jesus used to calm it—notably the security of Devon after the teeming hugeness of London, and Roger's insights and prayer over specific things which had happened to me early on. It took time for me to rebuild the fundamental ability to trust Christian people, but that trust proved foundational to any growth. Jesus expresses his love tangibly through his people on earth. I needed their arms, especially at the times when I could not feel his. I needed their loving words when my ears had become deaf to his voice.

But one of the root causes of my fear remained to be exposed and cut off. After I acknowledged that I had been abused, my old enemy leapt out at me again. Paralysed, stuck, helpless, vulnerable, terror striken—all these feelings gnawed at me from my gaping wound of fear. Many victims have expressed to me how acutely vulnerable they feel. Maybe this reflects the intensity of the helplessness they knew as children when their wills were violated. Today obessive fear no longer rules me. However, more recently I began to see something else. I had a certain need to control other people. I believe this sinful way of thinking comes from the root of feeling out of control. My abuser coerced me into a sexual act beyond my understanding. I never wanted to feel out of control again. So at school I would latch on the most popular girl in the class in an attempt to 'own' her. I did the same with Anna. Yet controlling others is yet another sin—in my case a bondage stemming from the wound of abuse, a bondage to be broken.

Even after I became a Christian, I wanted to manipulate people. Was all my evangelism, my spouting verses at people, a real giving out of love for them, or did I do it in order to fulfil a need in myself? I thought back in horror to the way I had dealt with David from the school for maladjusted children. I had needed that relationship as much as he did. In trying to become like God to him I let him down with tragic consequences. Though I had not caused his pain and though I wanted to help, looking back I can see that my own need of the relationship meant that I could not detach myself sufficiently. And I could not risk losing him by being honest about my own problems.

Because I can see the way I myself acted sometimes in the past, I am learning to beware of counsellors who are driven by their own needs. Sometimes counsellor and counsellee develop a wrong reliance on each other and hook in to control the other's behaviour. It can prove most damaging. One young man I counselled, back in Sidmouth, fell violently in love with me. I should have seen it coming, should have seen the way he leaned only on me. Again, I hope I am learning. Another time, I found myself beginning to feel attracted to a counsellee and recognised that an impulsive streak in me could land both of us in trouble. Being slightly more mature by this stage, I told my prayer group of my feelings. I chose to be accountable. But in the end I think that only my acute need of God held me back from sin, rather than any wonderful obedience. This song came out of the awareness of my vulnerability.

It was love kept me hanging on, and taught me how to
  come,
And only love left those chains on me so I'd never try to
  run.
My heart is like a wayward child prone to go astray,
And it's knowing that I need you, keeps me by your side.

Unless we are clear about seeing people through
God's eyes, wanting only the best for them with pure,
Christ-like love, things will go wrong. Any form of
manipulation within churches can wreak havoc.
Today I have no doubt that certain people within my
father's church suffered from wounds connected with
the fear of rejection, which festered until they drove
them to pull the church apart. Love means recognis-
ing the dignity of another human being and allowing
him or her to make a free choice, just as God allows
us to do, at whatever cost to himself and his Son.

The workaholic also may be driven by his need for
love and affirmation and by his inability to receive
either, but a third trait I have noticed in people who
have been wounded by fear works the opposite way.
The vulnerability they feel causes a kind of learned
helplessness. If the church put on a production of
Winnie the Pooh, they would fit the part of the sad
donkey, Eeyore, who always expected the worst.
'Oh, of course, it's not worth praying for me, God
will never give me this gift. He'll give it to all of you,
but he won't give it to me.' I expect you know the
sort of thing. Sometimes those who refuse to take on
responsibility exercise a weird form of control.

One of Jacob's computer games has PacMan
characters who for ever chug back and forth across
the screen, munching up everything in their path.
They can never have enough. Eeyores remind me of

love munchers, needing constant reassurance, because they refuse to accept love at its face value. However much everyone pours into them, somehow—munch, munch—it disappears without trace. Their sensitive antennae then pick up others' irritation, but they have set up the very rejection which they feared. They slide into introspective self-pity, thirsting for acknowledgement, while programming people to reject them more. I wrote the song 'River' for Eeyores—and we all feel Eeyorish at times, since we live in an imperfect world where human love will let us down. But God called us by name from the beginning. He loved us and wanted us, he appreciates us and he has plans for our lives. That truth will set us free from the fear of rejection, for only the great, unending river of God's love can satisfy the bottomless well of our needs.

I know you feel rejected, I know you feel starved of love,
There's a bottomless well in the centre of you that nothing
    can ever plug...
Let me take you to a River that will not run dry,
Dynamited in a barren land, when a man lay down and
    died.
And if you drink at that River, you'll never thirst again,
Freedom for living, healing for pain.

After being abused I took vows that no one would ever hurt me again. Later I had to break those vows in the power of the Spirit. Other vows guarded my sexuality and I had to break those too before I could give my whole self. I had never appreciated the power of words, both positive and negative. God created the world by speaking. Words which we speak can free us or put us behind bars. I had made vows thinking to protect myself, but in reality they controlled me and kept me in prison.

I felt vulnerable when I began to dismantle those 'word-bars', but if Jesus chose to make himself vulnerable in order to help people, then we must too. Only as I allowed God's living word of truth to rule and protect me did I find a new freedom. I began to discover the possibility of loving as he loves. Even today, if I feel threatened I find it easy to assume a 'confident professional performer' mask which prevents my relating honestly to people. More important, it can stop me saying what the Holy Spirit wants me to say to them. Strange how our strengths, the areas which God has dealt with, can become our weaknesses. I appreciate all God has done to help my confidence during public appearances. Where once I shook with panic attacks, now I have become oh, so professional—but it can work against me. For example, quite recently I sang to an audience of around a hundred prisoners. The men eyed me hungrily—a female! I braced myself, thought, 'I can cope!' and switched on my cool performer routine. I had a good talk worked out for that prison chapel, and the men listened, but I could tell that my words were not reaching behind their defences. Then, right in the middle, the Holy Spirit whispered to me, 'I want you to sing, 'Can I really be safe with you?'' In it I ask the audience:

> Can I really be safe with you?
> If I let down the mask that I wear
> If I'm open, honest
> And say how I feel
> Do you promise to accept what is there?

For I want to give myself to you
But I feel afraid of what you might do
If I open up my wounds to you
One cruel word would send me running for cover
And I might never come out again…

I had an on-the-spot argument with God over
whether or not I would obey him and sing that song
to a roomful of hardened criminals—and guess who
lost? So I drew a deep breath and said, 'I'm going to
take a real risk here, because this song tells you about
how vulnerable and wounded I feel sometimes. It's
going to hurt me if you smirk now, because when I
was young a man did something to me which wasn't
very nice at all. I have good reasons to feel defensive
about letting myself be vulnerable with men.'

I sang it then, all the way through. In the silence
which followed I said, 'I can tell that some of you feel
every bit as vulnerable as I do. In this environment
you daren't let on or you'd all kill each other. But I
risked making myself vulnerable to you because, in
the privacy of your own cell, I want you to make
yourself vulnerable to God. Be real with him. Let
down your mask and your defences.' And I read
them the passage from Isaiah 61 about how Jesus sets
the prisoners free and opens the eyes of the blind. A
strange stillness came over that chapel and, as the
men filed out, many shook hands with me. They even
made eye contact so that when they muttered,
'Thanks!' I could see they meant it. On that occasion
I won through and resisted the knee-jerk reaction to
play safe. Jesus, when wounded and abused, hung on
the cross. He was acutely vulnerable, but still honest,
still giving of himself. In doing so he drew at least

one other criminal being crucified to trust him, just
as he has drawn so many of us since.

When I tried to live the Christian life on my own I
failed dismally because I tried to control my relationship with God. Though later I let go, God often takes
me on re-runs to see if I will pick up the reins of my
own life again. For example, when I found out the
date the hospital had scheduled for my kidney operation I launched into a brilliant impersonation of a
school prefect. Steve and other close friends tell me I
tend to adopt this persona when I feel under pressure
or out of control. I started making lists. I cooked food
for the freezer. I contacted friends all over the place
and organised relays of them to take over running
our house and looking after our children. Some even
changed their holiday dates to fit my plans.

Shortly before the operation, I found out that the
hospital had no bed for me. They gave me a new date
for admission so, undeterred, I started my lists and
phone calls all over again. Would you believe the
same thing happened a second time? My pile of cards
collapsed. Only at that point did I stop to ask God
about it. I had been trying to round up his provision
for me and for my family.

There's nothing wrong with planning. People with
a different nature from mine, those who suffer from
learned helplessness for example, might need to learn
to plan more. But I tend to grab the reins to make up
for the fact that, for years, my life went spinning way
out of control. On this occasion God was asking me
to let go a little. Steve has a head on his shoulders. So
have my friends. The next few months hardly proved
the most pleasant or stress-free time of our lives, but
we survived.

God can use the dynamics of a present situation to
unearth hurts from the past, and to deal with them.
Sometimes, when I feel like I'm breaking up inside, I
ask God, 'Why?' But I have come to see that our pain
and loss—our 'death'—is precious to him. He stores
up all our tears in his bottle—and only bottles things
worth keeping!

> I hear a cry deep inside,
> The unhealed hurts of a wounded child,
> Wasted years and unshed tears,
> And facing your pain is the hardest thing to do.
>
> But precious to me is the death of my saints,
> Don't you know you're on holy ground?
> When the lake of pain has been fully drained
> I'll lift you and feed you and bring you to life again.
> I love you. I'm near you. I'm here.

One huge surprise has been living by faith. Steve
and I always thought that was for real saints, for
spiritual giants made of a different stuff from mere
mortals like ourselves, but we soon found out differently. After Steve lost his job in the sheepskin
business he went on the dole. Soon afterwards, I met
Marilyn Baker and she introduced us to her manager. He liked my music and, after offering me a
contract to record *Healing Stream*, also mentioned that
he had just started a management company and was
looking for people with some kind of ministry, rather
than just talent as musicians. It seemed the perfect
answer. The company would make our bookings,
and Steve and I could travel together, assured of a
regular income.

As soon as we had the first tour planned Steve

signed off the dole and we spent a happy six weeks touring with a group called Love Light. Then the management and recording companies both went bankrupt and the recording studio would not release more than the first rough mix of *Healing Stream* since they had not been paid. My heart had gone into that tape, perhaps more than any of the others, since I had written it as my gift to hurting people. We eventually released it as the first mix and, despite its technical imperfections, I received wonderful feedback from it. People have been filled with the Holy Spirit while listening to *Healing Stream*, some have found physical as well as emotional healing. One person wrote to me and said that, as she played it, she listened to the Lord for the first time in years.

However, all that encouragement filtered back to me much later. When the companies failed, so did our financial security. We asked the Lord what on earth should we do? In the end we felt that we should fulfil the bookings we already had and only continue after that if more bookings (and money) came in. Eight years later we are working on that basis, still 'living by faith'—which means living on the edge. But our initial step out of visible financial security proved the most frightening and exhilarating. I expected to wake up the next morning feeling like a cross between Mother Theresa and Joan of Arc, but found I still had to live with good old Lou Lewis.

Fortunately, God's faithfulness, rather than our faith, keeps us going. Sometimes his provision for us seems lavish. He kept us supplied right through my pregnancy, even when I put my back out at the beginning of ten days' ministry at one church. At other times things seemed dire and if we worried too much we would have had nervous breakdowns by now. We are learning to hand the responsibility back to the Lord, and he often allows us to teeter on the brink. From my perspective as a reasonably organised person, he often seems late. For example, one April we had no events booked all month and we needed to pay some urgent bills. Right at the very last minute a cheque arrived for the exact amount, with a letter which explained how God had asked the sender to give £500 the previous November, but had only now released him to send it to us. I felt encouraged for weeks!

In some ways, the longer we live by faith, the easier it becomes, because we can look back to so many times when God has rescued us from some emergency. The temptation, because each time looks slightly different, is to wonder if God is really up to this one. When driving through Wales we laughed about the many chapels bearing the curious name of 'Ebenezer'. Later we found out that the word comes from the Hebrew of the Old Testament, and means, 'Up to this point the Lord has helped us'. When the Israelites saw God accomplish something for them, often they put up an altar to remind them and their children and to build their faith. I began to see that each challenge could present an opportunity to grow. So many times the Lord has said to me, 'Learn the lesson now, or I may need to repeat it.' My song 'Never Be Broken' was inspired by these thoughts, and by the Psalms of ascents, which I love. They start by being real about the fact the Psalmist feels under intense pressure and end, as his faith level rises, with a cry of triumph to the Lord.

It's time to raise my Ebenezer, though it makes me smile.
I have done a thousand things but in faith I'm still a child.
Here I stand alone and empty, wondering where you've
gone.
Deep inside some stubborn hope keeps me hanging on!

I don't want to break your heart, I know I'm slow to learn,
May you find my lamp still burning, feet still standing
firm.
Father, Father, help me to see,
Father, Father, you're caring for me.
Promises spoken will never be broken.

I had baulked at the thought of starting a family
and then, just as Jacob was about to go to school,
Steve wanted to discuss our having another baby.
Yes, I loved Jacob and felt so grateful that we had
him, but I also looked forward to leaving him safe in
the classroom. Then I could enjoy time away from
the constant demands of a toddler, and space in
which to exercise my artistic, creative side. In the
end, I had to come to the conclusion that, for some
strange reason which I could not fathom, God
wanted me to conceive again. When our daughter
Cassia was born, it was love at first sight. I just had
to laugh and cry and admit that God had been right
all along, that he knew the best for me! Mind you, I
needed that very special bonding to Cassia—she had
me up three or four times a night for eighteen
months. God certainly has a sense of humour!

Jesus keeps making me see that, though I may feel
out of control, he is in control, not as one who would
abuse or reject me, but as one I can trust with
everything. Because he has convinced me that I am
worth something to him, I can allow myself to be

vulnerable in his presence. And, because he is restoring my own sense of self-worth, I can be vulnerable with others. I can laugh at myself, knowing that I'm not perfect. I can share my weaknesses as well as my strengths. It is amazing what that can release. I suppose Christian speakers usually talk about things which the Lord has taught them. On one church weekend I talked about things which I had failed to learn. At one point I happened to comment that I meet many vulnerable women in churches, women who are crying out to the Lord for safe men, who will treat them in a Christ-like way and not be abusive. Something happened in that meeting. Many of the men wept. I think, because I had been real, they started being real too. And, the last I heard, the lessons of that weekend have remained effective in people's lives.

Abuse and deprivation damage the will and it takes time to repair because habits and a whole way of life are involved. People whose wills have been made passive by various traumas may suffer more easily from compulsions. I have battled to give up cigarettes. Earlier, I succumbed to drugs which, in their turn, further blunted my will. Others struggle with over- or under-eating. But, if our human will can be weak and bound, also the will of Christ can live in us. I pray, regularly, 'Thy will be done'— especially when all my old sins seem to return to haunt me. Then, from a deep level, I know the truth—that I do want God's will, and his way.

18

Counselling

I'll make you a sower, even though you feel afraid,
For people are dying without my word of life;
They have pain but no place for their trouble,
And their good times fade with the passing of each day...
Love for the lonely, bleeding with a broken heart,
Healing and restoration where people have been torn
    apart...
Give it away!

During the four years the Sheldon Theatre Group
was in existence at times I felt that God was speaking
clearly to me, and at others I could have been wad-
ing through thick fog. Those around me commented
that writing songs seemed to help me work through
various issues in my life. Then I heard that my songs
dealing with people's hearts and hurts often had the
power to reach right through and help people with
similar needs to my own, so I began to slot more of
this kind of thing into my evangelistic concerts. It
seemed to have great impact if I spoke openly about
some of the things I had been through and of how the
Lord had helped me. Someone said, 'It's refreshingly

honest to hear someone tell it like it is, not how they think it ought to be!'

After I had worked through the problems caused by separation anxiety I helped Dr Roger Moss as he gave some informal talks. Following on from this, a Christian holiday camp called Royal Week asked if I could take some seminars for them. In three morning sessions I talked about my personal search for wholeness and, for the first time in public, I mentioned my lesbian affair. Many people came up to me afterwards. Most of them had been involved in homosexual activity of one kind or another and had never told anyone about it. Shortly afterwards an equally honest article about me in the magazine *Christian Family* had a similar effect.

Through feedback from the chuches who organised my concerts and from the various individuals who came to talk to me afterwards, I began to realise that God was using me to help heal the deep wounds of Christians, as well as to reach out to those who did not as yet know him. I began to offer to take seminars for Christians at the churches which sponsored my evangelistic concerts. My songs seemed to break through the dams of denial of other abuse victims, in particular. They needed more than a quick prayer at the end of the session, so I would suggest that they saw a counsellor. Or, if they lived locally, I might ask God about seeing them myself on a regular basis.

I had been counselling informally for some time. From the Sheldon prayer group I had learnt the value of talking and praying at a deep personal level, and later I started to meet with a few more people on this basis. One of the girls felt a long way from the Lord at first, but today she's my best friend and herself involved in counselling. Another who met with us then suffered deeply from depression, whereas today she is strong enough to take needy people into her house and to care for them.

I find that the public and private parts of my ministry complement one another. Counselling keeps me down to earth and helps prove the staggering claims I make in my songs, that Jesus can help hurting people. I find great pleasure in watching a person change, especially when, after a long process, someone finds her place of usefulness in the body of Christ, hears God herself for the first time, then reaches beyond her own pain to help others.

I have received great personal help through those who have counselled me, but people do not always understand why a person might need this level of help. Let me try to explain. When I had that pain in my kidney I popped round to the chemist for some paracetamol. When the problem kept recurring I visited our family doctor. She could not deal with the problem in her surgery so referred me to a specialist in our local hospital.

Recently, Steve took the drama one stage further, when Exeter hospital sent him by ambulance for a special scan at a better equipped centre in Plymouth.

I find this analogy helpful when considering spiritual and emotional health. Friends within my church—for example, my house group—represent the chemist. Their love and care and prayers have seen me through many a problem. Then a smaller group of mature Christians, praying together, might equate to the GP—often able to diagnose (and pray) about the root of a problem. They will be honest with me and I can be accountable to them, taking the 'medicine' they prescribe. It's great if someone with deep problems has those two levels of help in place, because both groups will provide vital support while the process of healing takes place, even when the person needs to be referred to the specialist, the counsellor. And even the counsellor, who can pray with authority into the situation, may need to hand the patient on to other specialists, other 'hospitals'.

I come into contact with so many hurting people whose needs will not be fully met by one seminar from me or by any one-off sermon, prophecy or prayer from the most godly person in the land. It saddens me to find so much need and so few people to help. We need to take counselling much more seriously.

I would love to see every church with a trained counsellor, maybe full-time, with a team under them who, after basic training, begin to specialise in certain areas. Various Christian agencies run courses and secular agencies, such as Relate, also train in some of the skills. (In some parts of the country, Christian counselling falls below the high standards of the secular variety, so I do sometimes refer those seeking help to secular agencies albeit with sadness.)

I'm writing the rest of this chaper for people who feel that God might be asking them to begin to counsel, so other readers may want to skip the next few pages. First of all, I would encourage those who are thinking about counselling. Don't reach beyond yourself at first, but start where I did—by befriending people, listening to one another and praying together.

Apart from one Leanne Payne conference I have no formal training, though I am looking forward to doing some when Cassia starts school. So please do not consider what follows in any way a guide on 'how to counsel'. Much of my counselling has been that peculiar, potent mixture of spiritual intuition and practical common sense.

Even the most eminent psychiatrists can give no simple formulae to help people overcome the effects of the various problems which mess up their lives, especially as individuals differ so much. Over the years, however, I have noticed that some ways forward work more effectively than others. Mainly, though, I try to be sensitive to the counsellee and, above all, to the Holy Spirit.

First, I have to build an environment in which the hurting person will open up. I would think it fair to say that establishing trust goes 90% towards helping. By the time they get to me, many people might as well flaunt a badge proclaiming, 'I'm a problem'. They need to hear that I don't see them like that, nor will they shock me by anything they reveal. Because they often hate themselves, I find them watching me for any evidence of rejection and I have learnt, even in my body language, to express, 'You are safe here. I love you and accept you for who you are.' When someone listens it does so much to free an individual. I try to listen, not only to the facts about what happened, but to draw out the feelings which have been buried so deep that they have never been expressed before.

I like to establish some ground rules before we start, making it plain that I cannot always meet a counsellee's needs or be there for her, because my travelling schedule and family demands often render me unavailable. I make it clear that I have many faults and still struggle in certain areas, because I think counsellees need to know that I am human too—although many secular counsellors disagree and deliberately keep themselves at a distance. Paul said in 1 Thessalonians 2:8 that the apostles 'were delighted to share with you not only the gospel of God but our lives as well'. It has certainly helped me when my counsellor has allowed her own humanity to show through.

It's important too that counsellees know from the beginning that I am not their last resort. I hope that I can help people in some measure, but many problems lie beyond my experience and I may need to refer them to someone else. I would always do this in the case of serious involvement with the occult, cases of schizophrenia or other psychiatric disorders, or anywhere I felt out of my depth. After all, a student nurse would not attempt brain surgery!

There is also the vital issue of confidentiality. I cannot carry all burdens alone, and so I reserve the right to tell Steve, or one female prayer partner. I make it clear that I can trust both absolutely not to gossip the persons' deepest secrets around the neighbourhood, even in the guise of 'prayer requests'.

Over the years I have learned to avoid situations where I control the counsellee or vice versa. Maybe I am growing more confident in the Lord's sovereignty so that, even if I begin to see something, these days I wait until the person sees it too. Sometimes, abuse victims feel helpless and like to be told what to do, yet God longs to free their wills so that they can make their own decisions again. I try to work around the deep longings of their hearts, rather than imposing any plan of mine on them.

When the only warmth in someone's childhood came from her abuser she will often sexualise other relationships in which care, love and concern are shown. Christians often mention the dangers of one-to-one counselling between men and women—without realising the potential for same-sex involvement, even where there has been no previous history of this. Ideally, we should counsel in pairs, except that the chronic shortage of counsellors makes this a pipe dream. I also feel that some kind of supervision of the counsellor is just as vital in the Christian as it is in the secular world, but due to lack of personnel this is not practicable in every area of the country. I find it invaluable if the counsellee has a good friend who is prepared to give her time. She can sit in on the sessions and help her friend through the rest of the week as well.

It can be hard to balance intuition and common sense. I have seen churches where a superfluity of 'words of knowledge' bind people up, rather than set them free. But then again, God's specific word can short-cut months of work by piercing to the root of the problem. When I first started counselling I would go up every avenue, but I suppose experience has taught me to recognise some of the fundamental issues which affect people and also to trust my gut feelings about which area to pursue and which may prove a red herring.

Occasionally I break my own rules. At a church quite recently a woman came up to me after a concert saying, 'Do you remember me?' I tried not to look as blank as I felt. She continued, 'It must have been a couple of years ago. I'd been told I couldn't have children. You prayed for me and prophesied that the Lord would give me a baby.' My heart sank. What must I have been thinking of? Prophecies like this, which did not come true, could cause huge problems for people. However, the woman smiled as she said, 'I just wanted to show you this!'—and disappeared. She came back into the church beaming, 'Here's our baby!' and handed him over for a cuddle. That wonderful moment just goes to illustrate that all my rules and safeguards cannot box God in.

Having established trust and the basis of our relationship, how do I try to help a counsellee to talk about things which she has kept bottled up? I have found that oblique methods such as drawing can help a victim distance herself enough to begin to get in touch with her barricaded emotions. Or I use the Psalms, whose strong emotions can reach into people's feelings without threatening them. Once I suspected that a woman had been abused by her father, but I could not penetrate beyond her good memories of him. But as we chatted about her wider family, the truth emerged, much to my relief!

Jesus used pictures and story scenarios to communicate with his hearers simply, yet on a deep level. The imagination, if led by the Holy Spirit and used carefully, is such a powerful tool that I believe it must be one of the most untapped resources in the Christian church. We shy away, quite rightly, from evil fantasies which may lead towards sexual or occult dangers. But if those things are Satan's counterfeits, they represent poor perversions of God's good gift of imagination. Used according to his purposes, with the Bible as a yardstick and accountability with others for checks and balances, it can work wonders.

So, for example, if someone tells me that she is stuck, I ask, 'What does 'stuck' feel like? Are you in a locked prison? Or moving forward in a fog, but unable to see your way? Or drifting on a raft in mid-ocean with no rescuer in sight? Ask the Lord to show you.' The person might reply, 'I'm in a fortress,' I ask if she can see any sort of doorway. She notices a raised drawbridge. I ask what is stopping her from lowering it. She feels threatened—the fortress is under siege from outside. I ask, 'Who are your enemies?' And gradually the whole problem begins to unfold. I find this method helps because the person can begin to get in touch with her deep emotions and buried trauma through something 'out there'. I'm by no means saying that all counsellors should use this way, just that I find it helpful. When the front door is locked and the key lost, a roundabout way in is better than none. For example, a person may not feel able to face the memory of a particular man, but perhaps could 'see' him as a particular animal in a zoo.

Also, I have begun to see the difference between praying *for* and praying *into* a situation. I used to spend time helping people talk through their problems. Then we would pray about those things, and that helped, because God often stepped in. But I find that, if the person can get in touch with their feelings about the problem (either through symbols or more directly) then we can invite the Lord into the situation and see him heal the feelings as they come to the surface, as well as deal with the other consequences of the problem.

Sometimes, before the wall of denial collapses, no progress appears to be made. The suffering person could not feel more numb if an iceberg encased her. Though God is beaming the sunshine of his love to melt the ice; though hammer blows of prayer have begun to crack its hold; the person herself feels nothing until the last frozen piece slides away. At other times, someone who appears to have his life reasonably in order goes for counselling and appears to come out worse than when he went in. His church promptly writes off the counsellor, but they need to bear in mind that before a problem can be dealt with it needs to surface, which can result in mess or even explosions.

As a counsellor, I have made mistakes and said inappropriate things. Ocasionally, eager to help, I have bitten off more than I could chew. Not every story ends happily and I only hope I learn for next time. At least, with all I have been through, I do have a sense of compassion and would run a mile from dumping all the blame for any failure upon the counsellee. It is also simplistic to blame the counsellor for every failure. The mix of personalities might not work, or the counsellee might not be ready to go further. I pray for any whom I can no longer help, that God will so order their lives to provide for their rescue in his way and his time.

Perhaps because I've learnt to be careful about whom I take on, I find that I can help most people along the path at least a little. I'm overjoyed to see deep changes in some to the point where they themselves are able to access fresh resources from Jesus in case of future hurt. I would love to see the time-span of the healing process reduced and pray that my music, public speaking and counselling will all work to this end.

But counselling will always take time. If Gordon, for example, had tried to pressure me, he would have set me back months. I have noticed that if I set a limit to the number of sessions available to someone, they progress far more slowly than if I make it clear that they can go at their own pace. The healing of deep wounds by Jesus' love works through a process, not an event. Given time, truth and love will make even a stronghold of evil loosen and finally disappear.

Can abuse ever be healed? Can innocence or a lost childhood be restored? Not completely, I suspect. Serious abuse leaves a scar which may not totally disappear this side of heaven, yet I have seen scars become less sensitive. They may hurt if put under too much pressure, but most of the time they do not control the way the person lives. Ultimately I want to see people no longer limited by their wounds and bondages, but able to use past experiences as they reach out with Jesus' love to others. Then their pain will become productive, rather than purely undermining. Some of the people I counsel have been through such things that they can only find any value in their suffering if they can come to a place where they give help and hope to others.

19

The Beggar and the King

I understand your dreams, for I go dreaming too,
Sometimes I face the pain, sometimes turn on you.
But I am just the same, a beggar searching for the King,
Praying you'll hear me sing upon my journey

I'm surprised how few sermons I hear on how Christians treat people. Some of our social skills are appalling and I'm sure few of us stop to consider the effect which our words have. From watching Steve smart I've learnt how rarely church people compliment those who work behind the scenes, and how often they criticise. Steve likes it when we work for television companies. They know the value of both technicians and managers. In fact, we joke that they treat him better than they treat me. But, seriously, I wonder how many other people find more affirmation outside the church than within it?

Once I had a twenty-minute slot in a church service and, since I would be singing as well as speaking, the Vicar gave the choir the evening off. Two elderly female choristers obviously objected to some young upstart taking over their role with her amplified sound. They insisted on appearing in full robes in the choir stalls and glowering at me, like bats, throughout the entire service. I count it as one of the greatest triumphs of my life that I resisted the temptation to turn round and stick my tongue out at them.

Another time Steve spent several hours of a sweltering afternoon setting up our PA system in a church. The choirmaster then appeared and said that he would have to move it all, because it was blocking the door through which the choir would process.

'Could you not come through this other door? It's only a few feet down the corridor!' suggested Steve, sweetly. But no, they always made their entrance through the one particular door, and so Steve spent another hour lugging heavy equipment round and re-running sound-checks, which neither of us found very funny at the time.

Steve's an unsung hero, laying down his life to serve me and others. We're a team. Not only would my work grind to a halt without his practical support, but I need his spiritual strength to buoy me up when I'm flagging, or to haul me back from zooming off into unreality in the excitement of the moment. People in churches sometimes ask Steve, 'What's your ministry, brother?' When he told one man, the reply came back, 'Yes, but what's your real ministry?' Surely, we are all only called to serve. My serving, being out front, carries its own reward. I'm sure Steve's will be all the greater in heaven but, in the meanwhile, how about a word of encouragment for all those beavering away behind the scenes?

Over recent years I have found myself taking seminars on various subjects, principally on wholeness and self-esteem, plus a few on sexual abuse. I find these both daunting and rewarding. Invariably, ten minutes before I start, the devil reminds me, in glorious technicolour, of the holes I fell into during the previous week. 'Who on earth am *I* to talk about *this?*' I mutter to myself, while searching wild-eyed for an escape route. However, in calmer moments I realise that self-esteem has to do both with who we are and who we are becoming. It's not enough to say, 'Well, I know that I'm not very nice, but Jesus accepts me as I am!' I have good reason for not liking some of my attitudes and actions, so I also need to know that God has the power to change them.

Sometimes people look at me askance when I start talking about self-esteem and wholeness, because adherents of the New Age have these things as their goals. However, there is a world of difference. Jesus said that we have to lose our lives in order to find them. In other words, we don't find the end product by looking for it. Jesus defined eternal life as 'knowing God' and we can only find our true selves in relationship with him. (You will understand that I certainly had quite enough of trying to find my 'self' apart from him!) Today my dream is no longer to 'find myself' but to hear the word of God and to obey it, for in that path lies fullness of joy. Self-esteem and wholeness come as by-products.

The paradox continues, for wholeness in the Bible does not mean total got-it-togetherness. Indeed that spiritual giant, Paul, said that when he was weak, then he was strong, because God's strength is made perfect in our weakness. I think of 1 Corinthians

10:12, 'So, if you think you are standing firm, be careful that you don't fall!' If I ever reached a place of complete wholeness, where I lived in some kind of permanent rosy glow, I might become quite a pain! In addition, unlike those who look for the 'god within themselves', a Christian, no matter where he starts on his journey, has someone to help. A friend once said, 'Jesus has always been with me, supporting and guiding me on my journey, even when he had to push me in a wheelchair!'

As we begin to ask God to show us ourselves, we find not only bad things which need redeeming, but the wealth of good and wonderful things which God has given to each one of us. And he made us all different! Steve and I have read a really helpful book about the Myers-Briggs indicators, which explain different personality types. What a revelation, especially when Steve and I discovered we each fell into opposite categories!

Lou—borderline   introvert: Steve—strongly extrovert.

Lou—intuitive: Steve—concerned with facts.

Lou makes decisions based on how they will affect others: Steve decides on the basis of logic. Lou likes to live in a fairly structured way with each day mapped out in her diary: Steve prefers spontaneity.

None of these ways of living is right or wrong— each has strengths and weaknesses and, ideally, we should balance each other. Now we understand a bit more, when we react to things in different ways I need no longer assume that Steve sets out to annoy me. If we both stop and think, we can see how our different reactions spring from the rich diversity of the different personalities God made.

Now I understand Steve better I realise that I spent years trying to turn him into a counsellor, whereas he has never shown a real interest in the way people tick. We need to accommodate our different personalities. After a weekend giving myself in concerts, seminars and personal counselling, I like to flop down and watch some mindless television, or maybe devour a light novel. Extrovert Steve, who has slaved away serving me in practical ways all weekend, is dying for a chat and some human company. We found ways to compromise once we appreciated one another's needs.

This new understanding also helped quite recently when we had to drive to Aylesbury for a concert. A church there had worked hard on publicising the event and we had let them down a couple of months earlier, when heavy snow had prevented us from travelling. This time our van developed a catastrophic fault 75 miles from home. Steve, the practical, logical thinker, decided the RAC's 'One Way Recovery' would tow us back to Exeter where a friend could fix the van cheaply for us. As a heart-decider, I felt appalled at this suggestion. How could we let the church in Aylesbury down again? No, we would have to ask the RAC to tow us there.

At one time, our difference of opinion would have led to a blistering row. But because we each understood our different ways of seeing things, when I pleaded with Steve, he agreed to trust me on this occasion. While watching for the RAC, believe me, I prayed, 'Don't let us down, Lord, or I'll never hear the last of this!' We did our concert in Aylesbury and were introduced to a friend of a friend of a friend. This man normally worked as an army mechanic in

Germany, putting vehicles back in action when they broke down in the middle of manoeuvres. He spent the whole of Sunday fixing our van so that we could drive back to Exeter.

I write this final chapter with a strange mixture of feelings—pleased to have reached this far, but with something gnawing at my stomach, muttering, 'You've implied more than you can deliver, Lou! They'll all be expecting such high standards of you now—and you know you'll never keep it up!'

Without doubt, God has done many things in my life. He's repaired much damage caused by events and behaviour patterns in my past. In other areas, though, I remain a complete fruit cake. For example, ask me to drive our van down the motorway and you'll see me do a disappearing act in the other direction. Or, on the way to some concert venue, I might engage in an argument with Steve which leaves me feeling as spiritual as a dish rag.

While telling my story I have tried to say, 'Please take me as I am!' If you were to arrive on my doorstep tomorrow I might greet you warmly, listen to you, help you even. But I hope you believe me when I say that, if you came at the end of a hard week you might see me struggling. But instead of being disappointed I hope you would reach out and give me some comfort, out of all that God has done for you.

Certainly the Lord has touched me, as I hope he has touched you, taking us further and further towards holiness. Yet, because he himself is pure light, paradoxically the nearer we come to him the more we see all that remains to be done. The devil, trying to make us give up, loves to whisper, 'See how

far you have to go!' But when God gave the Promised
Land to the people of Israel, he did so by stages, one
battle at a time. As it says in Deuteronomy 7:22,
'The Lord your God will drive out those nations
before you little by little. You will not be allowed to
eliminate them all at once, or the wild animals will
multiply around you.' In other words, it would have
been easy for God to help the Israelites to conquer
the land all at once, but he did it gradually, so that
they learnt to keep and rule it properly. Had everything come to me at once, I could not have controlled
all the new territory I held. Now my hope for the
future seems less foolish because of past battles
fought and won, in God's strength and timing. I am
learning to sing with both honesty and hope,

I'm just a pilgrim..though I sometimes make my home
Where all that glitters is not gold, and hearts are turned to
    stone;
Just a pilgrim, travelling this land,
Finding the rock of life underneath the sand.
Ever onward, ever upward, run the race that lies before
    us.
Here we have no lasting city, but we look for that to come.

I don't want to make it sound too easy. Every time
God has helped me press forward into new areas,
immediately beforehand he took away all that I
thought I had gained. Jesus said that the branch
which bears fruit will be pruned, but I find pruning
comes as a shock after a time of fruitfulness. Another
reason for difficulties can be that in trying to bring
hurting people in touch with God's healing love,
opposition may come from the enemy, because I am
fighting to take away the ground he has gained.

God takes us seriously when we pray for holiness, or try to help others at a deep level. We can go through some deep waters in the course of his answering our prayers. Steve and I have experienced God sifting our lives in every area. Even today, at times I feel like we are coming apart at the seams and wonder how we have the nerve to reach out to others. We have gone through huge difficulties even during the writing of this book. But when I think about the Christians I most admire, all of them have gone through dark times—and still do, on occasions. If we haven't been healed of everything, we do have the Healer, which is far more important. And God still chooses to use us, even when we feel under dark oppression ourselves.

In conclusion, I find myself thinking about one of my more recent songs, one of the very few which is addressed to myself.

It's taken me years to find you. When first I saw your face,
You were broken up and torn apart and out of sorts with
 the human race,
Running around in circles, trying to avoid the pain,
Crawling out into the light, for you heard you could be
 whole again.

It's taken me years to find you and now I see what you
 are,
You're very weak and very strong, very healed, very
 scarred.
But I'm bringing you into the open for all the world to see,
For I'm learning to love the heart of you, learning that you
 are me.

Over the years, hurtful things caused me to build defensive walls around myself, until God began to dismantle them gently brick by brick, a little at a time. The process has not finished. I am both strong and weak, healed and scarred. In five years' time I may see things differently from the way I see them now. I do hope so, because I long to learn more and more—about God, about myself and about other people.

I'll finish, not with words I have written, but with some from John Newton's hymn, 'Amazing Grace'. They say it all.

> Through many dangers, toils and snares
> I have already come;
> 'Tis grace hath brought me safe thus far,
> And grace will lead me home.

References and Copyright Details

All songs are by Lou Lewis, and the copyright of Zimrah Music, unless otherwise stated. Lou's music cassettes— *Don't Hide Away, Walls, Healing Stream, Victim* and *Private Lives*—can be obtained by mail order from Zimrah Music, 39 Union Road, Exeter, Devon, EX4 6HU, England. Telephone (0392) 439923.

Chapter 1: 'I'm No Hero' from *Walls*

Chapter 2: 'Jacob's Song' from *Walls*. 'Broken Heart' from *Healing Stream*

Chapter 3: 'Jacob's Song' from *Walls*

Chapter 4: 'Love has Let Me Down' from *Victim*

Chapter 5: 'Forgive Me' from *Private Lives*

Chapter 6: 'Love has Let Me Down' from *Victim*

Chapter 7: Title song from *Walls*. 'Hard Times make you Strong', by Jamie Owens, copyright Lexicon Music, 1975. 'Too Many Times' from *Gold* by Meet Jesus Music

Chapter 8: 'Feet on the Rock' from *Healing Stream*. 'Open my Eyes' (Not recorded)

Chapter 9: 'Knowing that I Need You' from *Healing Stream*. 'Tapestry' from *Don't Hide Away*

Chapter 10: Title song from *Don't Hide Away*. 'I Feel Lonely' from *Healing Stream*

Chapter 11: 'Broken Heart' from *Healing Stream*. 'I Know Where You're Coming From' from *Healing Stream*. 'Broken Heart' from *Healing Stream*. 'Jacob's Song' from *Walls*

Chapter 12: Title song from *Victim*. 'Valleys' from *Healing Stream*.

Chapter 13: Title song from *Walls*. 'I'm no Hero' from *Walls*. 'Substitute' from *Private Lives*. 'River' from *Private Lives*

Chapter 14: Title song from *Healing Stream*. Ibid. 'I Believe in You' from *Victim*

Chapter 15: 'Father I Forgive Him' (Not recorded)

Chapter 16: 'Valley's' from *Healing Stream*. 'None but Christ can Satisfy' by J McGranahan, Charles M. Alexander Copyrights Trust. 'Pilgrim' from *Private Lives*

Chapter 17: 'Tapestry' from *Don't Hide Away*. 'River' from *Private Lives*, 'Breaking Up' from *Healing Stream*

Chapter 18: 'Give it Away', from *Walls*

Chapter 19: 'Pilgrim', from *Private Lives*. 'Song to Myself' from *Private Lives*. 'Amazing Grace', by John Newton

Further Reading

Ryan, Dale and Juanita *Rooted in God's Love* (IVP: UK, 1992, by arrangement with University Press, Illinois)—a must for anyone in the process of healing.

I have found all Leanne Payne's books very helpful, especially the following:

Payne, Leanne *The Broken Image* (Kingsway Publications: UK, 1988 and Crossway Books: USA, 1981)

Payne, Leanne *Crisis in Masculinity* (Kingsway Publications: UK, 1988 and Crossway Books: USA, 1985)

Payne, Leanne *The Healing Presence* (Kingsway Publications: UK, 1990 and Crossway Books: USA, 1989)

Payne, Leanne *Restoring the Christian Soul Through Healing Prayer* (Kingsway Publications: UK, 1992 and Crossway Books: USA, 1991)

Allender, Dr Dan B *The Wounded Heart* (CWR: UK, 1991 and NavPress: USA, 1990)—I warmly recommend this book as the most helpful I have read on the subject of sexual abuse.

Sandford, Paula *Healing Victims of Sexual Abuse* (Victory House)

Shepherd, Grace *Aspects of Fear* (Darton, Longman and Todd)

Chave-Jones, Myra *Living with Anger* (Triangle)

Crabb, Lawrence *Inside Out* (Scripture Press)

Pytches, Mary *Yesterday's Child* (Hodder and Stoughton). This book includes an excellent list of counselling services in the UK.

McRoberts Ward, Ruth *Self Esteem, Gift from God* (Baker Book House: Grand Rapids, Michigan, 1984)

Murray, Andrew Any general titles (various publishers)

Nee, Watchman *Sit, Walk, Stand* (Kingsway Publications)